Organizing Independence

To my mother and father

Organizing Independence

Negotiations between Journalism and
Management in News Organizations

Elena Raviola

*Torsten and Wanja Söderberg Professor in Design
Management, Academy of Art and Design and Director of
Business and Design Lab, University of Gothenburg, Sweden*

Edward Elgar
PUBLISHING

Cheltenham, UK • Northampton, MA, USA

Cover image: 'Communication, Advertising and Progress' by Giulio D'Anna.
Permission to reuse the image was kindly granted by Leogalleries in Monzo, Italy.

Published by
Edward Elgar Publishing Limited
The Lypiatts
15 Lansdown Road
Cheltenham
Glos GL50 2JA
UK

Edward Elgar Publishing, Inc.
William Pratt House
9 Dewey Court
Northampton
Massachusetts 01060
USA

Paperback edition 2023

A catalogue record for this book
is available from the British Library

Library of Congress Control Number: 2022931079

This book is available electronically in the **Elgar**online
Business subject collection
http://dx.doi.org/10.4337/9781802200379

ISBN 978 1 80220 036 2 (cased)
ISBN 978 1 80220 037 9 (eBook)
ISBN 978 1 0353 1347 1 (paperback)

Printed and bound by CPI Group (UK) Ltd, Croydon, CR0 4YY

Contents

Acknowledgements

The long and slow writing of this book has been the subject of many conversations and selfish moments of isolation over the last years. Undoubtedly my family, friends and colleagues are happy to move the conversation forward and to finally see the "book" printed. This project has been dependent on the contributions of many people whom I would like to thank: my colleagues for helping me with access to the fieldwork (more details in the chapters); all the funders for generous funding—in particular the Hamrin Foundation, Wallander and Hedelius Foundation and Torsten and Wanja Söderberg Foundation for Design Management; all the strong and independent women for mentoring and coaching me endlessly, invaluably and always gracefully; my news-aholic husband Claes for always listening and for his incurable idealism. Above all my parents. This book is dedicated to them.

1.   Is media independence under threat?

> A news outlet, it is a whole. Shareholding structure, financing sources, and content are a whole package. A medium, even before it writes or says anything, is an address, a promise. The press of the Resistance [after World War II], Sartre's Libération, the free radios, all these media born of a fight and carried on by a generation were first of all promises. The wave of the pure players[1] of 2007 is the most recent one. *Rue89*, like *Mediapart*, like us, like others, every day more numerous, have carried and carry the promise of a press which is liberated from the technical constraints of the old supports (it will continue), but also liberated from the old connivances with the journalistic trade association (body), with the political powers, with the money, with the advertising, in short with what we call establishment. (Schneidermann, 2011)[2]

> In what other organization but the newspaper are the managers not allowed to tell the employees what to do? (A top manager of a major Scandinavian bank that had just become shareholder in a major Scandinavian media group in a conversation with me about organizing news production, Autumn 2014)

As Sam Dolnick (2018), Assistant Managing Editor at *The New York Times*, wrote, the task of the media as the "watchdogs of democracy" is to "find out new facts and uncover things that someone doesn't want you to uncover" for the public good. Many business and political leaders fear headlines on the front pages of morning newspapers or the opening of the evening TV news show because they know that a media scandal may mean the end of their careers. As Ed Hutcheson, Managing Editor of the newspaper *The Day*— .k.a. Humphrey Bogart in *Deadline* (1952)put it, "[t]hat's the press, Baby. The press! And there's nothing you can do about it. Nothing!"

Examples of politicians and corporations, however, trying "to do something about it"—to paraphrase Hutcheson—re several in recent years. The image of the former President of the United States of America, Donald Trump, shouting at journalists, accusing them of producing fake news and attacking practices that are commonly considered appropriate if the press is to play the role of the Fourth Estate is a known one. At the end of November 2018, Hungary's Prime Minister completed his plan to place the media under his control, as many private news outlets were "donated by their owners to a central holding

---

[1]   Online-only news organizations were called "pure players" in the 2000s. *The Huffington Post* is often cited as an example of a pure player.

[2]   This is my translation from French. I have translated all the qot es from French, Italian, and Swedish that appear in this book.

company run by people close to the far-right prime minister" (Kingsley, 2018). In Russia, the privatization of state-owned media companies contributed to the dismantling of the journalistic professional community and the deterioration of its ethical standards, as most news outlets have become means of propaganda in the hands of the president-friendly oligarchs (Roudakova, 2017). The well-known Los Angeles Times (LA Times) scandal is another example. On 10 October 1999, the LA Times published a supplement on a new sports arena in the city, and it was later revealed that it had earned more than 2 million USD in advertising revenue from publishing it, as the revenues were split between the newspaper and the sports arena.

Independence has long been one of the core values of news producers (Vos & Singer, 2016), but it is not an uncontested principle. As the same Ed Hutcheson reflected, "A free press, like a free life, sir, is always in danger" (Brooks, 1952). The international association Reporters Without Borders (RSF, Reporters Sans Frontières, n.d.), which publishes a World Press Freedom Index annually, has recognized this situation, making media independence one of its key mission points:

> RSF defends the independence of journalists and media from political and corporate influence, conflicts of interests and every other kind of pressure. It makes specific legislative proposals with the aim of improving national laws affecting the media, and it seeks to reinforce international norms that protect journalistic freedom and independence vis-à-vis all political, corporate and religious centers of power and influence.

In this statement, political, corporate, and religious centers of power and influence are identified as the ones from which the work of journalists should be protected. Yet in their review of what scholars mean by media independence, Karppinen and Moe (2016) noted the relationality and situatedness of the concept. They discovered that independence may be talked about in relation to various entities (the media system, media organizations, journalism, or individual voices/speakers) from various organizations (the state; political parties; special interest groups; market forces; and major media corporations, which are often referred to as "the mainstream"). Media independence can be guaranteed by various means: laws and statutes; organizational arrangements; or self-regulation, ethical guidelines, and professional culture.

Independence, thus, functions also as a critical principle in news organizations, which frames and justifies the way in which work is organized, responsibility is regulated, and the company is financed and managed. In different settings and times throughout history, though, this principle has been practiced in various ways and has formed a variety of organizational forms. Media studies have consistently acknowledged the existence of dualities in media organizations (Achtenhagen & Raviola, 2007, 2009; Picard, 2002; Tuchman,

1973, 1978; Tunstall, 1971), or to see it from the institutionalists' perspective, the co-existence of different institutional logics within the media (Friedland & Alford, 1991; Thornton & Ocasio, 2008; Raviola, 2010; Raviola & Dubini, 2016). Media scholar Julianne Schultz has named the media a "bastard estate", referring to the uniqe standing of the press as a political institution whose success is measured commercially (Schultz, 1998, p. 4). In such a "pluralistic context" (Denis, Langley & Rouleau, 2007; Jarzabkowski, Matthiesen & Van de Ven, 2009), independence has been interpreted in a variety of ways and is practically negotiatede– very day, but also in not-so-everyday circumstances.

This book analyzes how independence has been organized and practiced in three news companies. Following the tradition of organization studies of the media (Engwall, 1978; Boczkowski, 2005; Czarniawska, 2011), thus, this book approaches the media as organizations and, as a way to understand independence in practice, it holds a particular focus on how the relationship between journalism and business management has been conceived, contested, and negotiated. In this book, *journalism* is understood to be a professional practice serving the democratic function of holding the powerful accountable to the public, and *business management* refers to efforts to make profit by increasing revenues and/or decreasing costs. In all three news organizations described here, digital technologies played a key role for a number of reasons:

(1) In the field discourse about the financial difficulties of newspapers and their death, the Internetove r the last ten years, specified as "the tech giants" like Google, Facebook, Appleha s been held responsible for cutting both readership and advertising figures. (See, e.g., *The Economist*, 2006.)

(2) Digital technologies have made new ways of producing news possible, by changing relationships with sources and allowing interactions with the readers, for example.

(3) In a wider wave of digital ventures, entrepreneurship has also increased in journalism, primarily in online news. As Briggs (2012, p. xxi) put it, while long being considered "a public service, more of a calling than a profession", now journalism "is also a business opportunity".

The aim of this book is threefold:

(1) I want to demonstrate not only the variety of meanings that independence acqi res in the field and over time in a news organization, but also the complexity of the fair, every day, and the not-so-everyday work performed by journalists, managers and entrepreneurs to uphold and update independence to current challenges. This fair work goes far beyond the traditional and virtual "Chinese Wall" between the newsrooms and the business rooms that much of media studies used to take for granted.

(2)   By focusing on organizing, I want to shed light specifically on how
       journalism and management ideals get compromised, yet simultaneously
       actualized in everyday organizational life. My methodological attempt
       here has been to depart from what is done in news organizations, rather
       than analyzing norms and beliefs on what should be done.
(3)   I want to emphasize the various roles that objects and things (whether
       technological or not) play in various organizational compromises: car-
       rying inscriptions, and thus stabilizing compromises between journalism
       and management, while simultaneously betraying them.

MEDIA INDEPENDENCE IN THEORY

The notion of media independence is grounded in the constitutionally protected freedom of speech (Jones, 2011), which was forged intellectually,
legally and practically in the wave of the Enlightenment, the revolutions of the
1700s and their long tail in the 1800s. As historians recognize, such freedom
is entangled to the Gutenberg invention of the printing press, which "made
the soil from which sprang modern history, science, popular literature, the
emergence of the nation-state, so much of everything by which we define
modernity" (Man, 2010, p. 14). A common metaphor used to refer to the Press
and its freedom is that of the Fourth Estate. The origins of the expression are
debated and have been attributed by many to Edmund Burke on the opening
up of Press reporting of the House of Commons of Great Britain, based on
Thomas Carlyle's reporting on his "On Heroes, Hero Worship and the Heroic
in History" (1893/1993). Burke would have said that "there were Three Estates
in Parliament; but, in the Reporters' Gallery yonder, there sat a *Fourth Estate*
more important far than they all" (Carlyle, 1893/1993, p. 141). Carlyle goes so
far as to eqa te printing to democracy:

> Printing, which comes necessarily out of Writing, I say often, is eqi valent to
> Democracy: invent Writing, Democracy is inevitable. Writing brings Printing;
> brings universal everyday extempore Printing, as we see at present. Whoever can
> speak, speaking now to the whole nation, becomes a power, a branch of govern-
> ment, with inalienable weight in law-making, in all acts of authority. It matters not
> what rank he has, what revenues or garnitures. the reqi site thing is, that he have
> a tongue which others will listen to; this and nothing more is reqi site. The nation is
> governed by all that has tongue in the nation: Democracy is virtually there. (Carlyle,
> 1893/1993, p. 141)

In his earlier book, *The French Revolution: A History*, Carlyle (1837/2006)
had already talked about the Fourth Estate, which "of Able Editors, springs up;
increases and multiplies; irrepressible, incalculable". The notion of the Fourth

Estate insists on the press as an institution independent from the other three Estates and working in the public interest. As the American essayist Walter Lippmann (1922) claimed in his *Public Opinion*, the latter is a phantom, an abstraction, but nevertheless not an undesirable ideal, guiding efforts to overcome particular and individual interests to make news a sort of a public knowledge (Schudson, 1995; Ekström & Westlund, 2019).

The notion of the Fourth Estate, independent and working in the public interest, which denoted first the gallery outside the Parliament where reporters sat and documented political activities of the Parliament, acqi red a flexible meaning over the years, mainly bearing the idea of the necessity of media independence for a healthy functioning of democracy (Schultz, 1998). As media scholar James Bennett (2015, p. 2) has argued: "Media independence functions as a utopian vision of the media's role in society for those who regulate it, own it, work within it and even study it." Like other utopian visions, it seems to be a taken-for-granted necessity in democratic societies: Who would disagree about the centrality of media independence? Such independence is reqi red to guarantee the functioning of media as the Fourth Estate— he role of the press to scrutinize and oversee all powers in society on behalf of its readers, and ultimately of its citizens (Schultz, 1998). Conseqe ntly, compromising on media independence would mean compromising on democracy.

Jü gen Habermas is a sociologist who has devoted explicit attention to the issue of media independence, placing the independence of the media system in a central position in the deliberative democracy project that he valued highly (Habermas, 2006). Discussing the power structure of the public sphere, he distinguished four categories of power: political, social, economic, and media power. He maintained that, based on the technology of mass communications, the mass media are a source of power on their own, and that that power is exercised when the media "select and process politically relevant content and thus intervene in both the formation of public opinions and the distribution of influential interests" (Habermas, 2006, p. 419).

In Western democracies, the utopia of media independence is based on the conviction that media power is "innocent" (Habermas, 2006): "Journalists operate within a functionally specific and self-regulating media system. The relative independence of mass media from the political and the economic systems was a necessary precondition for the rise of what is now called 'media society'" (p. 149). Habermas suggests that deliberative legitimation processes in complex society function only with media independence, which implies that two conditions are fulfilled. One condition reqi res that media maintain independence from their environments—the political and economic systems— while simultaneously creating political communication between civil society and politics. The other condition reqi res mass media to offer citizens the opportunity to participate in and react to political discourse. "The latter condition is troubling, to say the least. The literature on 'public ignorance' paints a rather sobering portrait of the average citizen as a largely uninformed and disinterested person (Friedman, 2003; Somin, 1998; Weinshall, 2003)" says Habermas (2006, p. 420).

Habermas's reasoning on media independence should probably be treated as a grand idea or as an ideal type. When reading it, I felt like political scientist professor Daniel Hallin during his first encounter with a journalist. Hallin confessed that he was impressed by his interlocutor's "sense of wholeness and seamlessness in [his] vision of journalism, or to put it the other way around, the absence of a sense of doubt and contradiction" about the mandate to scrutinize power independently (Hallin, 1992, p. 14). But this "wholeness", seemingly universal and ever-existing, was the result of a specific historical process, as Hallin (1992) explained. In the 20 years between the 1960s and the 1980s, journalism, particularly US journalism, "had overcome all the basic contradictions that historically have troubled the practice of journalism", namely the dilemma of being part of the power system yet critically reporting on it. By performing objectivity and impartiality and reporting simple facts rather than taking stands in political debates and social campaigns, it became "possible for journalism to be independent of party and state and yet fully a part of the 'Establishment'" (Hallin, 1992, p. 14).

In the process of professionalizing their work, journalists had come to accept the professional norms of objectivity and neutrality as their highest constraints, and the hierarchy of the newsroom as the normal way of organizing news production. Hallin cited an investigation by Rothman and Lichter (1987), who compared their study of journalists' relationships with their editors with Leo Rosten's 1937 study. They learned that the journalists of the 1980s were less likely to lament editors' interference in their stories than were their counterparts of the 1930s. Rothman and Lichter (1987) interpreted this result as a sign of contemporary journalists' complete autonomy, but Hallin (1992, p. 15) saw it as an indication of undisputable internalization of the constraints on professional objectivity and impartiality that occurred over those 50 years.

At any rate, the reqi rements of journalists' objectivity and neutrality have fostered the idea of independence from primarily politics and economic powers. In what Hallin called the "High Modernism of Journalism", the journalists seemed "to be genuinely above politics" (Hallin, 1992, p. 15). Those 50 years witnessed the unprecedented growth of newspapers as well; they became large, mass-producing companies, looking for an impartial product that could appeal to a large mass of readers and consumers (Schudson, 2001). This was also the period when that "Chinese Wall" between the newsroom and the commercial rooms in news organizations was reinforced through codes of ethics and legislation, and, in practice, in the physical organization of work (Coddington, 2015). As Karppinen and Moe (2016) have noted, media independence was translated in many countries after World War II into the establishment of independent media authorities. These authorities would represent the arm's-length principle of the constitutional separation among legislative, judiciary, and executive powers in modern democracies.

The distinction between journalism and business is of core importance to journalists in news organizations and it considered crucial to the realization of the ideal of independence. Truth vs. publicity, journalism vs. advertising content, democracy vs. ownership interests, and public service vs. the market are some of the dichotomies defining independence in this industry. Thanks to prosperous newspapers, which strove to avoid everyday interactions and conflicts by separating the sacred (newsroom employees) and the profane (other employees), journalists have come to consider themselves "above economy"a– bove the economic and financial demands of their companies. As Hallin (1992) wrote, "Journalists could think of themselves more as public servants or as keepers of the sacred flame of journalism itself than as employees of a profit-making enterprise" (pp. 15+6) . During this era of High Modernism, journalists were prosperous and powerful; they became part of the establishment, while considering themselves perfectly independent of it.

About the same time that Hallin (1992) was identifying this paradox, Bourdieu (1992/1997, 1996) noticed that journalism was the locus of an opposition between two principles of legitimation, which he called pure and commercial. *Pure legitimation* is given to journalists who are recognized by their peers as highly competent, and whose values and principles internal to the profession[3] are beyond reproach. This process of legitimation through peer recognition is typical of fields of cultural production (Bourdieu, 1979); a good historian, for instance, is one whom other historians consider to be a good historian. *Commercial legitimation* is attained through numbers: The higher the numbers for revenue, readership, viewership, advertising, sales, and profits, the greater the recognition.

My observations of news production point at much more complex and therefore more interesting situations than those described by Bourdieu. Is the number of readers not used as a measure of the relevance and celebrity of journalistic work and an index for selling and pricing advertising? Is profit not understood to be both a measure of financial success and a necessity for maintaining independence? Journalism has never been pure (Raviola, 2014), although it has often reconstructed, and longed for, a fictional past in which purity ruled. Moreover, as Hallin (1992) noted more than a qa rter-century ago, even if one believed in that pure past, the era of High Modernism is over, as the two conditions that made it possiblepol itical consensus and the eco-

---

[3]   Or, as Bourdieu (1992/1997, 1996) would say, *field.*

nomic security of media industriesha   ve ceased to exist. The new era is characterized by a contestation of that taken-for-granted independence of the true or imagined yesterday. As Karppinen and Moe (2016, pp. 105-106)   claimed:

> ... the contestation over the meaning of independence is topical because of two tendencies. First, at both European and national levels, commercial media actors have actively sought to reframe the distinction between commercial and public service media as a choice between "independent" and "state" media. Second, the digital transformations and the decline of legacy media organizations have given rise to new actors as well as new aspects of control and dependence. As a conseqe nce of these transformations, the traditional line between journalism and advertising, for example, has increasingly become blurred by new forms of sponsored content. Furthermore, the increasing power of multinational news aggregators search engines and social networking sites has also reheated the qe stion of what we mean by media or journalistic independence.

What does media independence mean in practice today, when many types of organizations are increasingly mediatized, and when traditional media suffer from increasing economic difficulties? In my studies of news production, independence has been a recurrent theme in various contexts and circumstances, although it had never been the point of departure of my investigation. It made a strong appearance in my study of the largest Italian financial newspaper, in which I focused on the integration between online and offline news production, and how it had transformed professional practices of journalism (Raviola, 2010). This concept was not the point of departure of my investigation, but my interlocutors often mentioned it, and it seemed to catalyze a great deal of organizational energy, conflict, and negotiation. The debate around independence was probably one of the most fascinating debates of the field. In my later studies of a regional Scandinavian newspaper and a French entrepreneurial journalistic venture, my focus was on the ways they organized innovation, but shifted in both cases toward their striving for survival and the defense of their independence. Although I had heard the concept mentioned often in all the three settings, I was struck by the different ways it was framed and in the concerns raised by these different framings.

REORGANIZING NEWSWORK: INDEPENDENCE AND NEW TECHNOLOGIES

> In the face of digitalisation, new actors and the disruption of traditional competitive dynamics of media markets, legacy news media, including both public service broadcasters and newspapers, have gradually lost the unqe stioned, unchallenged status of "a fact of nature" in the digital age ().. . As a conseqe nce, they increasingly need to legitimize and reaffirm their position in the eyes of both audiences and media policymakers. (Karppinen & Moe, 2016, p. 108)

Much of the literature on the media crisis focuses on the difficulties faced by traditional news organizations in dealing with the present situation, leading to the layoff of many journalists and the death of newspapers. Digitalization is often accused of causing the erosion of the newspapers' traditional business model, producing information for readers and providing audiences for advertisers. In the field of journalism, however, not everyone despairs over the wave of digital technologies. The crisis of traditional news organizations has been the reason for two apparently opposite transformations of the news field: a wave of increasingly large media companies and an upheaval of innovative journalistic start-ups.

On the one hand, many newspapers have been acqi red or have merged into larger media groups, thus increasing the ownership concentration in media industries (Doyle, 2013). Although the big hope of cost saving through media convergence in gigantic media groups failed at the turn of the millennium, the mergers and acqi sitions of the 2000s, together with the multiplication of technological platforms, have led to explicit attemptsbot h on the editorial and on the business sidet— o realize synergies. For many, this has meant a reorganizing of newswork, in the way that several of the Swedish editors I interviewed called "working smarter", and introducing business models. As organizational scholar Barbara Czarniawska (2011) showed in her rich and enlightening account of everyday life in three European news agencies, newswork in the digital age of information abundance is a form of cyberwork, relying heavily on cybernization and cyborgization. The former implies that machines play an increasingly important role, the latter implies that the increasing dependence of humans on machines.

On the other hand, many new initiatives appeared with the goal of renovating news production and changing the old ways of financing journalism, without renouncing to the core journalistic principles and practices. At the beginning of the 2000s, in order to categorize these initiatives, the phrase "entrepreneurial journalism" was coined, often by journalists searching for journalistic recognition and economic sustainability. In 2016, Tim P. Vos and Jane B. Singer studied the framing of entrepreneurial journalism in the popular and trade press between 2000 and 2014: how it was defined, the tone of the discourse surrounding it, and which ethical and practical implications were discussed. They found no clear definition, but the term usually referred to journalist-founded enterprises delivering some sort of news online. In an often-cited article, Andrew Rice (2010) defined entrepreneurial journalism as pulling together journalism, technology, and business. Vos and Singer (2016) also discovered that most commentators writing on entrepreneurial journalism were talking about ventures that survive not only on the basis of two revenuesr— eaders and advertising—but many other sources of income: consulting, web design, and training, for example.

The tone of the discourse was generally positive, although some critical voices were raised. Little has been written about the practical and ethical dilemmas of entrepreneurial journalism. It seems that most practitioners thought of entrepreneurial journalism as the future of journalism, possibly saving the principles of journalism, while joining it with business. Vos and Singer, however, raised qe stions about the ethical and practical dilemmas involved in conflating the role of publishers and editors, as is the case with entrepreneurial journalism. They argued that the spread of entrepreneurial practices may have a significant impact on the field of news, which has been built around the conflict between the professional logic of journalism and the managerial and commercial logic, both logics possible through the separation of the roles of publishers and editors.

These new trends in the news field caused the reshaping of the way in which news production is organized, and a transformation of the relationship between journalism and management. Independence has acqi red new meanings and new practices—both in the legacy media and in new entrepreneurial media ventures. New voices and forms of journalism, financed outside legacy media organizations (e.g., through crowd funding and by private investors), take pride in declaring themselves independent of legacy media. The Internet joined in with a strong ideology of democracy, promising that "people" would be able to raise their voices like never before. All these developments contribute to the emergence of new meanings and new issues related to independence, which come from politicians and corporations, but also from established media companies and their consumers. It is the variety of these meanings and practices related to independence, particularly in the relationship between journalism and management, which are under investigation in this book.

STUDYING ORGANIZATIONAL COMPROMISES

Many organization scholars have acknowledged the fact that we live in a pluralistic world and have tried to provide a number of concepts to discuss and analyze this plurality. To mention but a few, Kraatz and Block (2008) spoke of institutional pluralism, Thornton, Ocasio, and Lounsbury (2012) introduced the concept of institutional logics, Cloutier and Langley (2007) reintroduced the concept of competing rationalities (Radcliffe, 1997; Townley, 2002), and Denis et al. (2007) spoke of pluralistic contexts. The relationship among different logics, rationalities, and contexts is often portrayed as a tension among various groups of people who identify with opposing ways of seeing the world. Many examples of these tensions can be found in studies of New Public Management or healthcare organizations. (See, e.g., Hammerschmid & Meyer 2005; Lindberg, Czarniawska, & Solli, 2015; Schedler & Proeller 2002.)

Traditionally, professions and management were assumed to represent opposing sides of this duality: on one side, the ambition of autonomy and public service; on the other side, the struggle for control and commercial success. (See, e.g., Engel & Hall, 1973; Sarfatti Larsson, 1977). As I noted elsewhere (Raviola, 2017), the ample sociological literature on professions and professionalization (Abbott, 1988; Freidson, 1986; Sarfatti Larsson, 1977; Scott, 2008) describes how professions define fields of expertise, provide their members with ethical norms, and prescribe what to do under various conditions. Yet the relationship between professions and management has become more complex because of the recent professionalization of management (e.g., Reed & Anthony, 1992), the transformation of professions in the audit society (Power, 1999) and the increasing technological standardization of professional work (Czarniawska, 2011).

As in other areas of modernity, the High Modernism of Journalism (Hallin, 1992) implied that objectivity is journalism's dominant norm, with independence being one of its supporting organizational principles. This understanding of independence sounds close to the understanding of Nature that Latour (2016) and his followers described as the distinctive feature of the modern faith. "We Moderns are terribly proud of the fact that we can think of 'nature' as it really exists, independently of any kind of culture or belief", wrote Debaise et al. (2015, p. 168, qot ed in Latour, 2016, p. 107): Journalists are indeed strongly fighting to uphold their independence from the realitypol itics, business, and so ont— hey are reporting on and in which they exist. This book is an investigation of the High Modernist dream of independence and its actualization in three news organizations.

Luc Boltanski and Laurent Thévenot (2006) offered an original approach to the study of plurality and pluralistic organizations, suggesting, as Jagd (2013) put it, an analysis of critiqe rather than a critical analysis (Raviola, 2017). In the words of Thévenot (2002b, p. 55), "we wanted to account for the way actors place value on people and things in ways that appear to be more legitimate than others"; to focus on these evaluations, which create "the linka— lways a matter of tensions—between the general and the particular"; and are oriented toward coordination, rather than being "pure a posteriori reconstructions". This approach has seemed particularly appealing to me, as it breaks the connection between a specific logic and a concrete group of people, representing it. After all, both management and journalism are constructed as lines of arguments to justify or disqa lify certain practices by a variety of actors. Boltanski and Thévenot's social world is "a space shot through by a multiplicity of disputes, critiqe s, disagreements and attempts to re-establish locally agreements that are always fragile" (Boltanski, 2011, p. 27), rather than the site of passively and unconsciously endured domination of one class over another. Their "six orders of worth" (inspiration, market, industrial, domestic, fame, and civic) have attracted great interest in organization studies.[4] Here, I am most interested in the process by which "disputes, critiqe s, disagreements" develop, and "always fragile" compromises are constructed, making different justifications and judgments of worth compatible.

My analysis is therefore focused on the practices of critiqe , justification, and compromise involved in the production of what comes to be called "news". According to Boltanski and Thévenot (2006), people agree by justifying the worth of their actions and decisions with reference to a higher common good. Through this process, conventions, which are working on the basis of a tacit or implicit agreement among individuals to participate in them, function both "as the result of individual actions and as a framework constraining the actors (Dupuy et al., 1989, 143; also Favereau, Biencourt & Eymard-Duvernay 2001, 238)" (Deqe ch, 2005, p. 469).

Although many scholars have claimed that agreement is necessary for coordination, I chose to join in David Stark's (2009) sympathy for tensions, conflicts, and disagreements as part, and perhaps even means, of coordination: "We can act in concert when we do not agree about why our actions are valuable" (Stark, 2017, p. 388). Further, encouraged by Czarniawska (2004) to focus on action nets rather than organizations, I studied what Bessy and Favereau (2003, p. 134) called *actions à chaud* ("hot actions"a– ctions in the making), and I analyze the disputes when and where they happen and the compromises when and where they are made. In the practice of coordination, disagreements represent occasions in which worth is tested. The link between the general and the particular common good, which is decisive for establishing worth, is qe stioned during tests. Such tests can be of two kinds and consist either of qe stioning the way in which a certain action instantiates a higher common good (test of state of worth) or of qe stioning the higher principle governing the situation at hand (test of order of worth). Tests can be temporarily resolved in compromises, in which people agree to come to terms with or at least suspend the dispute, without necessarily settling it, and are therefore ready to contest the compromise anew.

Building on Thévenot's conceptualization of organizations as "compromising machines", I have joined Jagd (2011) here in noting that "the notion of compromising work may be the major contribution" of the so-called French pragmatism "to the study of organizations" (Raviola, 2017, p. 739; Thévenot, 2001). In investigating how independence is practiced in three news

---

[4]   See e.g., Annisette and Richardson, 2011; Cloutier and Langley, 2007, 2013; Daigle and Rouleau, 2010; Denis et al., 2007; Fronda and Moriceau, 2008; Jagd, 2011; Hervieux, Gedajlovic and Turcotte, 2010; McInerney, 2008; Mesny and Mailhot, 2007; Patriotta, Gond and Schulz, 2011; Stark, 2009.

organizations, I use the term *organizational compromises* to describe how the relationship between journalism and management is organized there. I also analyze instances of contestation, failure, and sometimes the new life of these compromises in each of these settings. The term "organizational compromise", therefore, has a double meaning in my analysis: It refers to the ways in which compromises help to organize and frame work and how they are created by an organization with all its history and material arrangements.

The approach advocated here is similar to Actor-Network Theory, in that I postulate symmetry in the treatment of "central dichotomies of Western modernity such as truth/falsehood and nature/culture" (Guggenheim & Potthast, 2012, p. 261). Just like the production of scientific facts in Latour and Woolgar's (1979) laboratories, news production is not only a matter of interactions among journalists; the organizational compromises between journalism and management are not simply a matter of principle disputes between those who qa lify as journalists and those who q alify as managers. As Jagd (2011) wrote, the worlds are not abstract entities; they are polities made concrete in and with objects and subjects. Tests, disputes, clashes, and compromises are not merely discursive moves, but involve the material world made by objects and subjects, which intervene concretely as proofs to support critiqe s or justifications of given actions.

The world is full of objects, and although many of them usually stay in the background, somebody, in an act of justification, may sometimes bring some of them to the forefront. When this happens, objects are explicitly "qa lified", to use Boltanski and Thévenot's (2006) term, with the purpose of instantiating or contesting the worth of a certain situation or action. Still, as Thévenot (2002a, p. 192) has reminded his readers, "We assume that people can be qa l- ified in all the 'worlds', whereas objects are more easily attached to a single world". Yet my observations in the field revealed that the "attachment" of objects to one or the other world of worth is sometimes the actual focus of the contestation, and that organizational compromises may be inscribed in given material arrangements at one time and broken by these same arrangements at another time. Thus I chose to explore "a rival hypothesis", as Thévenot called it (2002a, p. 192) in a footnote— hat objects are also mobile and active in their attachments to different worlds.

THIS BOOK

This book is based on three field studies of news organizations in three countries: Il Sole-24 Ore in Italy, Stampen Media Group in Sweden, and *Rue89* in France. In what follows, I briefly describe these three news organizations and my original approach to studying them. In the following chapters, I use the phrase "making the news" to point at efforts to discover, evaluate, write, and publish news in the specific products of each case. The three chosen cases follow my research journey to investigate how newswork is organized in tradi-tional newspapers on their digitalization process and their accessibility results from a mix of opportunity, personal taste and rationale. Il Sole-24 Ore was my case of departure and first access. Since I am Italian and have graduated from a business school in Milan, I found starting my fieldwork in Milan and in a community that I could relate to (and that could relate to me) particularly appropriate. I observed there many practices that I recognized in my other case studies and at the same time I encountered specific incidents that raised my interest for how independence was practiced. In the spirit of a light com-parison, the next step was to choose another case to make sense of what I had observed in the first one. So, from the Southern European metropolis of Milan I went to Gothenburg, the second largest city in Sweden, where I worked, lived and spoke the language. I chose to study Stampen Media Group, which was interesting to my investigation because of its explicit digital efforts and of its growth business strategy. These cases showed similarities in the way news making was organized and technologies used, but not surprisingly— ee Hallin and Mancini's three models (2004)t— hey also showed many important differ-ences in the way independence was framed, more specifically with regards to the relation between journalism and business management. One of these dif-ferences was a much higher fluidity between the principles of journalism and of management and their communities. Following this trace and curious about a growing phenomenon that many talked about in the field, namely journalistic online start-ups (see Bruno and Nielsen, 2012), I asked myself what could happen when journalists became entrepreneurs. A chain of contacts brought me then half-way between Italy and Sweden, to the XX arrondissement of Paris at *Rue89*, together with Professor Pablo Boczkowski.

I have unidentified all my interlocutors and have assigned them gender-neutral names[5] in order to ensure their anonymity. Although this decision has prevented me from highlighting some key considerations about gender in the cases I studied, my priority was my interlocutors' anonymity, which could have been placed at risk had I identified their gender.

Il Sole-24 Ore and the Paper–Web Integration Project

Il Sole-24 Ore Group is a multimedia publishing company based in Milan, Italy, active primarily in the domestic market. It produces business news and

---

[5]   In the first case, the names are assigned in English, as very few Italian names can be considered gender-neutral. In the second and third case, the names are assigned in the language of the fieldwork, that is to say Swedish and French.

information intended for professionals through its various media: newspaper, news agency, radio, Internet, and professional publishing (magazines and books). The group is named after two smaller Milanese business newspapers that merged in 1965: *Il Sole*, which was founded in 1865; and *24 Ore*, founded in 1946. *Il Sole-24 Ore* became a mass newspaper that played a valuable role in a time of significant economic and social transformation in the country.

The flagship product, *Il Sole-24 Ore*, a salmon-colored broadsheet business daily newspaper, had a circulation of 334,000 copies[6] in 2008, according to the national official statistics of ADS (2008). Radio24, which was founded in 1999, reached a record listening audience of 2 million during 2008. The main news website, ilsole24ore.com, was launched in 1996, reaching over 3 million viewers in January 2008. Professional information is delivered through books, databases, other online services, and specialized magazines for lawyers and accountants.[7] The group also organizes training courses and produces software packages for various management purposes.

At the time of the study (2007-2008) , the group employed 1,400 people, of which approximately one-third were journalists. It was owned entirely by the Italian Federation of Employers until December 2007, when the group went public. Its value on the Milanese Stock Exchange was then estimated at approximately 750 million EUR. At the end of 2019, according to the group website (Gruppo24ore, 2019), the group employed 908 people and the shares were publicly owned at 38%, while the Italian Federation of Employers controlled 61.5% of them. In Chapter 2, where I discuss the case of Il Sole-24 Ore, I write about the company divided in two parts: Newsroom and Business, as my interlocutors called them. The Newsroom was the main site of news making and the place of work for journalists, editors, and graphic assistants. Business included such functions as marketing, human resources, and advertising, and also included top management. At this financial newspaper, the adjectives "editorial" and "journalistic" were reserved for work and products made in the Newsroom, and management and managerial-characterized Business.

When I approached the Il Sole-24 Ore Group in 2007, through a friend's contact with the Newsroom Secretary, I heard about the so-called integration project, which became my focus. It was a project aimed at integrating the newspaper and website news production, and through it I observed how the object of publication—paper or web—shaped and simultaneously sustained certain journalism practices. The analysis of my field material focuses on the

---

[6] Data from 2008, see ADS (2008). www .primacomunicazione .itwww.primaco-municazione.it

[7] *Commercialisti* is one of the Italian professions: accountants who specialize in a sector or sectors. Il Sole-24 Ore Group publishes different magazines for these different groups of *commercialisti*.

role of the objects in instances of contestation of the relationship between journalism and advertising.

Stampen and the Restructuring of a Media Group

Stampen Media Group was founded in 1988, when its newly appointed CEO, Peter Hjörne, third-generation successor in the family business, bought out the other minor owners of the local newspaper *Göteborgs-Posten*, which was founded in 1813 (Wedel, 2015). In 2005, Stampen then entered an expansion period, primarily comprising aggressive acqi sitions of other local newspapers in the country, through which it became one of the largest media groups in Sweden. The acqi sitions were financed primarily by large bank loans and motivated by the desire to be ready for the digital future. As Peter Hjö ne said, they undertook "a big responsibility for the development of mass media" in Sweden (SVT, 2015).

During the expansion period, Stampen was often hailed as a success at international newspaper conferences, and indeed seemed to have constructed a new way of surviving in the gloomy future that was facing newspapers. My study at Stampen focused on the development of new digital products, particularly at the newspaper, *Göteborgs-Posten*, in 2011‐2012, during the period of high optimism.

Growth came to a sudden stop in 2014. The 2013 income statement reported a total loss of 862 million SEK (~81 million EUR), ascribed primarily to the fact that goodwill assets of earlier acqi sitions were finally written off. From this time onward, the group has been struggling with its financess— hort of liqi dity and under pressure from the banks and the state to repay the loans. In May 2016, after being declared on the verge of bankruptcy many times, it finally filed for reconstruction, which is the last attempt to save a company.

In Chapter 3 I tell the story of the Stampen Media Group, based on accounts of journalists and managers during the expansion and media reports on the troublesome development of the company. This story shows how the agreed-upon organizational compromise seemed to submit journalism to management principles during the expansion period, promoting economies of scale and synergies. This compromise did not hold, however, as the company was held financially accountable by its creditors.

Rue89 and Entrepreneurial Journalism

Rue89 is a French news website, which started as a generalist news outlet, but now specializes in writing about the societal conseqe nces of the digital revolution. It was founded in Paris in the spring of 2007 by an engineer and four journalists from the newspaper *Libération*. From their blogging experience as foreign correspondents for *Libération*, three of the founding journalists had the conviction that the Internet could and should be used to revolutionize journalism and the field of news. Their main idea was to create a website that could be a tool for dialogue with the non-journalists"— readers and experts"i— n order to include them in the newspr oduction cycle. As journalists, however, they said that they wanted to "maintain the keys" of the production to control the news flow and its qa lity. Thus, they left *Libération* and launched www.rue89 .com.

The products and services offered by *Rue89* have grown significantly since its foundation. Along with several website developments in 2011 and 2013, *Rue89* also published a monthly print magazine between 2010 and 2011. And although the magazine eventually closed down for economic reasons, *Rue89* did launch applications for mobile and tablet during the same period. In an attempt to diversify the sources of revenues (advertising counted for about 65-70% of the revenues in 2011-2012) , *Rue89* engaged in a number of other activities. It instituted merchandizing , which accounted for a small percentage of profits, along with training programs, consulting services, and web agency services, which, altogether constituted about 30-33% of the revenues. The organization grew steadily. In 2007, a small team of full-time volunteers, including the founders and several young journalists, worked for the website and few consultancy services. By the beginning of 2011, when I started my study, there were about 25 full-time employees.

I tell the story of *Rue89* from its birth to acqi sition, focusing on the way in which journalism and management negotiated and compromised in everyday organizing. The study shows how the organizational compromise that had initially been agreed upon established the need to reach breakeven in order to be editorially independent, and how this situation held, despite contestation and negotiations all the way to the acqi sition, when it was broken and a new organizational compromise was established.

CONCLUSIONS

With the aim of analyzing and reflecting on how media independence is organized and thus actualized in practice, the three field studies analyzed in this book offer illustrations of three organizational compromises between journalism and management. These organizational compromises also realize three ways of understanding and practicing independence. The case of Il Sole 24-Ore can be presented as the case of "News vs. Money": The separation of the newsroom and the company (including all other employees) is physically inscribed in the architecture and practically sustained by everyday practices. Attempts to breach the wall, which are present both in paper and in online news production, are often interpreted in line with the overall organizational compromise of separation.

The case of Stampen, its growth and its reconstruction, illustrates a different organizational compromise between journalism and management. This is a case of making "News for Money": Profitability and the economic value of the company and its operations represent an overarching principle of worth, even over journalism. The credibility of the brand, which can be used to justify investments in journalistic investigations, is necessary for sustaining the value of the newspaper's immaterial assets.

The case of *Rue89* represents yet a third way of organizing a compromise between journalism and management. Their idea of entrepreneurial journalism was to make "Money for News"t— hat breakeven and profitability were considered key not for themselves, but in order to guarantee editorial independence.

The distinction among the three organizational compromises may oversimplify the complexity of the present and past of each of the cases analyzed here. It is important to mention it, however, for three reasons: (1) It renders the variety of ways in which media independence is organized and performed in practice in news organizations; (2) It shows the different ways in which news organizations have transformed themselves in the face of digital technologies, by focusing particularly on how the relationship between journalism and management has been reinterpreted in the digital era; (3) It highlights the practical and material stickiness[8] of the organizational arrangements, which result from negotiations between journalism and management and enact the compromises between them. These organizational arrangementsbot h material and practicale— onsist of such provisions as the way walls are placed, how products are designed, and how routines of communication are established between the newsroom and the business rooms. Such arrangements make independence possible in practice, while simultaneously compromising the ideals of journalism and management.

These compromises are organizational, both in the sense that they are made by organizations and in the sense that they organize work and worth. And, as compromises, they threaten the pure High Modernism[9] of media independence, but they also make it possible in practice and translate it over time.

---

[8]   By "stickiness" I refer to French science and technology scholar Bruno Latour's way of seeing materiality as carrying stability in the world: "Technology is society made durable" (Latour, 1990).

[9]   Here I refer to Hallin's (1992) definition of High Modernism: "an era when the historically troubled role of the journalist seemed fully rationalized, when it seemed possible for the journalist to be powerful and prosperous and at the same time independent, disinterested, public-spirited, and trusted and beloved by everyone, from the corridors of power around the world to the ordinary citizen and consumer" (p. 16).

2. Around the Chinese Wall: separating news and money

In this chapter, I explore how independence is organized in a traditional newspaper by focusing on a specific aspect of that independence. I investigate how journalistic content is made independent of advertising content in everyday newswork practices and how the separation between the production of news and the production of money—advertising money in this case—is organized and negotiated around a printed newspaper and its website. In the traditional newspaper business model, this aspect of independence has been particularly significant, and it has usually been discussed in connection with the journalists' autonomy and authority (Carlson, 2015).

Newspaper companies have long obtained their revenues from two sources: *advertising* and *circulation*—daily sales and subscriptions. Media economists have explained this double-revenue model as selling readers to advertisers, whose weight in the composition of income has varied across countries and publications (Picard, 2002). Under the principles of modern journalism (Hallin, 1992) and during the development of newspapers as mass products of the 20th century (Schudson, 1981), these organizational arrangements divided those who produced content (and thus readers) from those who sold the readers (to advertisers), as manifested in the news product. These arrangements were considered key in maintaining the professional norm of autonomy from business influences (Coddington, 2015), an autonomy that epitomized the ideal of an independent press (Maras, 2013).

The case of the Italian business newspaper *Il Sole-24 Ore* investigated in this study and discussed in this chapter presents a model in which journalistic autonomy—and defense against interferences over the profession's exclusive jurisdiction (Abbott, 1988)—was organized by separating money and news, business management and journalism, profitability and democracy as principles of worth, represented by different organizational communities and spokespersons. This is a story of the legendary "Chinese Wall" that exists between the newsrooms and the business rooms and its transformation in the shift to online presentations (Coddington, 2014; Carlson, 2015; Porlezza, 2017). For print newspapers, the number of copies sold every day corresponds not only to circulation revenue; it also affects the price of advertising, as it represents a promise of the consumer's reach for advertisers. When newspapers started launching news websites, the vast majority of news organizations gave free access to online news, thus limiting their stream of revenues to advertising. Advertising was sold primarily as a function of the number of clicks on the websitea— n approximation of online readersa— nd became a measure of both advertising revenue and popularity of the content in real time.

The separation between journalistic and advertising contents, which is highly valued in modern journalism (Hallin, 1992) has been inscribed in self-regulatory documents of journalistic and publishing associations in many Western countries. In Italy, the Charter of Journalists' Duties, signed in 1993 and agreed upon by the *Ordine dei Giornalisti, OdG* (National Committee of the Association of Journalists) and the *Federazione Nazionale Stampa Italiana* (National Federation of the Press) emphasized this separation, stressing the importance of signaling to the public the desire of the media to self-regulate. A paragraph on *Information and Advertising* explicitly illustrates this point:

> Information and advertising
> Citizens have the right to receive correct information, always distinct from the advertising content and not harmful to individual interests.
> In each case, advertising messages must be distinguishable from the journalistic texts through clear indications.
> The journalist must observe the principles established by the agreed-upon protocol on transparency of information and by the National Contract for Journalistic Work; he or she must always make the advertising information recognizable and must in all cases make it possible for the public to recognize the journalistic work as separate from the promotional message. (*Ordine dei Giornalisti*, 1993, p. 3)

At the time those words were written, this separation was considered a significant manifestation of journalism's independence from economic power, leading to the independence of the press. It materialized in a number of specific practices in established newspapers, like the clear distinction of advertising from journalistic content both textually and visually and the refusal to placement advertising for companies or products adjacent to articles mentioning them. For their part, advertisers have long been searching for innovative forms of communication that would be less easily distinguished from journalistic contenta— dvertisements that readers would not interpret as advertisements, and would be perceived as less invasive (McChesney, 2004; Carlson, 2015). Thus, new formats have appeared in print and online in which the boundaries between advertising and journalism have been blurred (Serazio, 2013).

At the beginning of the 2010s, a new term appeared in the media industry: "native advertising". It refers to sponsored content that is made to look as much as possible like the rest of the publication (usually a website), with no clear signals that it is paid advertising content. This type of content is considered particularly effective advertising, as it recreates "the user experience of reading news instead of advertising content" (Ferrer Conill, 2016, p. 905).

Even before the possibility of developing online native advertising (Wojdynski & Golan, 2016; Li, 2019), the introduction of sponsored pages and advertorials (texts promoting products or services in print newspapers that are written like articles and sponsored by advertisers) and the positioning of advertisements on the front page have raised concerns in newsrooms (Cameron, Ju-Pak, & Kim, 1996; Eckman & Lindlof, 2003; Brown, Waltzer, & Waltzer, 2001). The appropriateness and value of such content at the boundary between that which is editorial and that which is advertising has been negotiated and debated inside news organizations, in the field and in academia. These discussions have also been shaped by the new possibilities offered by digital technologies and by new practices established online within and outside traditional news organizations. Although not identifying themselves as journalists and not defined as doing journalism, bloggers and other influencers have, in fact, been at the center of the debate on the blurred boundary between newsworthy information and advertising (Pedroni, 2015; Boerman et al., 2018; Maares & Hanusch, 2020). Consumers' associations have raised the issue of trust and transparency of interests in relation to all information that is distributed.

In what follows, I describe in greater detail the first news organization I studied[1]—Il Sole-24 Ore Group— hen move on to describe and analyze various episodes of contestation, negotiation, and compromise concerning the distinction between advertising and journalistic content.

IL SOLE-24 ORE: A CLOSER VIEW

During the time of my study (see also Raviola, 2010), between 2007 and 2008, Il Sole-24 Ore Group consisted of five units:

- Publisher, responsible for the newspaper, the *24* magazine, and its side productsbooks or CDs sold with the newspaper.[2] (However, in Italy, the editor-in-chief is legally responsible for everything that is written in the newspaper.)

---

[1] I conducted this study during my doctoral studies. For a more extensive presentation of this study, see my doctoral dissertation (Raviola, 2010). Parts of the field study were also described, analyzed and theorized in other ways in other publications (Raviola & Norbäck, 2013, Raviola, 2014; Raviola & Dubini, 2016).

[2] Side products could be add-ons to the newspaper such as books and CDs sold with the newspaper, mainly to increase sales of daily copies. This strategy was popular in Italy in the early 2000s and contributed to a significant increase of newspaper circulation.

- Radio24, responsible for the radio and its website;
- Professionals, responsible for specialized publishing and training programs;
- Multimedia, responsible for online content and services; and
- System, responsible for advertising sales for the entire group.

The Group's production could be presented as:

- Over 50 journalistic products[3]
- 13 sites in Italy and 8 others around the world
- 10 printing plants, 2 of which are owned by the group
- 1,400 employees, 460 of whom are journalists[4]
- 511 million EUR in revenues in 2006, 572 million EUR in 2007, 573 million EUR in 2008, and 502.7 million EUR in 2009
- 50 million EUR earnings before interest, taxes, depreciation, and amortization deducted (EBITDA) and 16.7 million profit in 2006; 59.7 million EUR EBITDA and 27 million EUR profit in 2007; 47.9 million EUR EBITDA and 16 million EUR profit in 2008; and 6.5 million EUR EBITDA and 52.6 million EUR profit in 2009.[5]

Over the years, Il Sole-24 Ore Group had grown, not merely in size, economic results, and audience reach, but also in the prestige and relevance of its journalism. On 6 December 2007, in an official presentation of the company made for the Initial Public Offerings,[6] there is talk of an Il Sole-24 Ore model "– of competence, depth and balance which has become over time a great asset of credibility and authority" (Il Sole-24 Ore, 2007, p. 8). This model is based on an integrated, multimedia, editorial system, which aims at "daily delivering facts and comments, as an economic, financial and political compass" (Il Sole-24 Ore, 2007, p. 8).

Many of the journalistic products are branded under the Il Sole-24 Ore umbrella. The products created internally (not resulting from the acqi sition of another organization, like the news agency, Radiocor) have "24" in their name,

---

[3] It is noteworthy that they specify "journalistic products", to distinguish them from their non-journalistic products. The journalistic products are those published by journalists. Journalism in Italy is a nationally regulated profession.

[4] As some of the journalists noted, the ratio of journalists to administrators is lower than 1 to 4. This is considered too low by many journalists, as they see administrators (i.e., everybody not working in the newsroom) as representing bureaucracy, as opposed to the journalistic work on the content of the products.

[5] Revenues, EBITDA, and profit are the official figures reported in Il Sole-24 Ore Group *Annual Financial Report 2007, 2008, 2009.*

[6] From the Merriam-Webster's dictionary: "An initial public offering (IPO) refers to the first time a company publicly sells shares of its stock on the open market" (https://www.merriam-webster.com/dictionary/initial%20public%20offering).

to identify them with Il Sole-24 Ore. The radio station, for example, is called Radio24 and the free sheet is called *VentiquattroMinuti* or *24'* (24 Minutes). Thus, the various units are to be thought of as a family: the *24s*.

Headqa rters is located in the northeastern area of Milan, some 6 km or eight stops on Metro Line 1 from Milan Cathedral. Il Sole-24 Ore Group relocated to the new building in 2004, in a move that combined all parts of the organization. The new building, inaugurated in 2007, was designed by famous architect Renzo Piano, who, a few years later, designed a new building for *The New York Times*, modeled after Il Sole-24 Ore. The dominant material in the so-called new "lighthouse" is glass, rendering the building easily recognizable among the surrounding buildings. Glass has a symbolic function for the newspaper as well, as a journalist wrote in the monthly newspaper magazine when the building was inaugurated:

> The glass windows and walls are symbols of the editorial group, which delivers the image of a moving light above the stone and still city. The electric light passing through the glass symbolizes an architecture that lives day and night. (Maugeri, 2003, p. 30)

In official documents, the lighthouse was described as being "aim[ed] at reflecting the new nature of the digital empire" (Renzo Piano Building Workshop, 2004, p. 37) and as making "the arcane life of a newspaper journalist less hermetic to the metropolitan audience" (p. 36). The building is impressive indeed, and, as Andrea, an old-timer journalist told me one of my first days at the site, "It's a good building for official meetings, and represents the greatness of the newspaper, especially compared to the previous location."

The separation between journalism and management is inscribed in the physical space of the building, in organizational documents, in the news products, and in the organizational discourse. Il Sole-24 Ore's managers represent what they call "The Company" and its journalists represent the Newsroom— two areas of responsibility that should not interfere in each other's work. The Newsroom consists of all the journalists, designers, and assistants of various kinds who are housed on the second and third floors to the left of the elevators, and the Company consists of everybody else.

As Alex, Head Editor of the weekend financial supplement *Plus*, put it during a lecture at Bocconi University:

> The organization of the Newsroom must be separated [from the Company]. This is a conseqe nce of the norm reqi ring a separation between journalistic and advertising content. There can't be a precise and effective distinction between journalistic and advertising content if they are blended in the organizational structure. (Financial journalist, Bocconi University, Milano, September 2007)

If the norm is to be effective, then, it must be inscribed in the organizational structure, in which responsibilities and work practices must be clearly distinguishable. To make things clear, he drew on the blackboard the organigram of *Il Sole-24 Ore*. I was in the audience and was able to reproduce it in Figure 2.1.

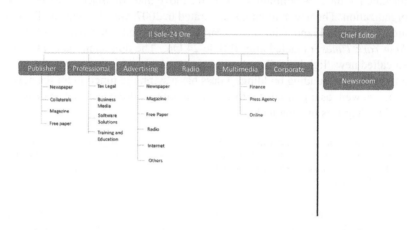

Source: Author.

Figure 2.1   *My reproduction of the drawing made by the financial journalist from Il Sole-24 Ore in a class at Bocconi University, September 2007*

The thick black line between Newsroom and Business signals the division of responsibilities: Newsroom personnel answer and report only to the editor-in-chief, and the editor-in-chief responds only to the readers; the managers of the various Business divisions answer and report to the CEO, and the CEO responds to the shareholders. This division of responsibilities is inscribed in the newspaper, which reports every day on the names of the people responsible for the Newsroom content and for business issues.

The imaginary wall between Newsroom and Business rooms cannot have windows or doors. I asked one of the editors about the possibility of changing jobsof   moving across the wall.

Elena: Even a person working on the other side of the wall, in marketing or advertising for example, can't move over [to the Newsroom]?
Taylor: No, as far as I know, this can't be done. The personnel department, perhaps, but advertising or marketing, not at all. Maybe a certain kind of marketing,

but when you have to deal with products, with companies, they are sources. ().. The advertising department doesn't give a damn about the newspaper [about keeping the newspaper clean of interference from advertisers]. It only has to collect money, and it would sell its mother, if needed. In contrast, we [the Newsroom personnel] never have to sell ourselves for anything. In other words, if you have to give bad news about a company, you give it and that's that [even if it is an advertiser]. They are, so to speak, two different mentalities. Doing advertising and being a journalist are two different things. (Interview with Taylor, an editor, January 2008)

The separation between business issues and people on the Business side and journalism matters and people on the Newsroom side is enacted in everyday practices and inscribed in the materiality of the newspaper. In their production of print newspaper, journalists work independent of the Business side, though there are established practices to allow the necessary communication across the divides.

The organizational structure of the Newsroom contains a special position for managing the interface between journalism and business issues. A journalist with the title of Newsroom Secretary is in charge of such practical issues as organizing the journalistic personnel and the everyday newspaper operations, which necessarily involve contacts with various business managers. The distinction between news and advertising is also inscribed in the physical newspaper, in which there is a visible distinction between journalistic and advertising contents. The design of the newspaper pages includes both journalistic and advertising content, however, with spaces negotiated throughout the day by an editor and an advertising person, whereas the rest of the Newsroom simply receives the pagination resulting from such negotiations.

ORGANIZATIONAL STRUCTURE OF THE MAIN NEWSROOM

The main newsroom delivered three main products: the newspaper, *Il Sole-24 Ore*, with all its supplements; the main website, ilsole24ore.com, and other related websites; and the monthly magazine, *Ventiquattro*. This newsroom was located on the second and third floors of the building and, according to the architect, the space should have been organized as open space. The idea of openness and transparency was not fully embraced by the Newsroom personnel, however, and the open space was converted to closed rooms for each product section, with some open areas in the middle for the assistants. The rest of the second and third floor was divided into rooms for the various sections of the newspaper and a separate large room for the news agency. Between the rooms are islands, as they are called in the newspapera– reas where the graphic assistants sit and design the pages, search for pictures, and draw tables and graphs.

Between 60 and 80 graphic assistants worked in the Newsroom at the time of my study, all of them in Milan. These employees are polygraphists and graphic designers. Some of them, called graphic journalists, are responsible for the overall layout of the products and of some special graphic features. I call them all graphic assistants.

Between 250 and 300 journalists also worked in the Newsroom. Approximately 200 journalists were located in Milan; some 50 journalists worked in Rome, and a few others worked around the country and around the world.

The *Il Sole-24 Ore* Newsroom operated under the direction of the editor-in-chief, who was responsible for every product coming out of the Newsroom and for the contents of all these products. The Newsroom was structured like a pyramid: The editor-in-chief was on the top of the hierarchy; three vice-editors-in-chief followed, followed in turn by the central office employees: central office editors[7] and the newsroom secretary. The rest of the Newsroom was divided into *newsrooms* (*redazioni*), corresponding to six sections of the newspaper (Finance, Internal Affairs, Foreign Affairs, Law, World, Culture), plus the online newsroom.

Newsroom personnel sometimes describe its structure as similar to that of the military or the feudal system.

Each of these newsrooms had its own hierarchical structure, with a head editor (*caporedattore*). Next in line are the vice-head editors (*vice caporedattore*); then come two or three desk editors (*capiservizio*); followed by two or three vice-desk editors (*vice capiservizio*); and, finally, the reporters (*redattori ordinarii*). These hierarchical levels corresponded to the most freqe nt journalistic career path at the newspaper. Each of these employees was in charge of "desk activities", as the journalists called them, overseeing "the daily cooking in the Newsroom" (Interview with the online vice-head editor), like distributing and editing texts and coordinating colleagues.

A career path alternative to deskwork was that of "writing", as journalists call it. At any point in their careers (usually at qi te a high level, perhaps even when they are head editors of a section), some journalists decided not

---

[7]   Central office editors are five journalists who have assumed the role of coordinating and performing the overall editing of the newspaper before printing—which includes headline adjustment. The art director also worked in the central office, supervising the overall graphic design and selection of visual elements of the newspaper. "Journalist" is the most generic category of those working in the newsroom with textual elements of the newspapera— category that includes editors, reporters, and correspondents.

to do desk activities and devote their time to reporting news and writing articles. These journalists are officially called *correspondents*. The decision to be a correspondent excludes the journalist from the section's hierarchy and creates a direct reporting relationship to the editor-in-chief. Correspondents are usually highly specialized; their signatures are both valued and prestigious. They are considered privileged, as they do not need to attend to the bureaucratic procedure of producing a daily newspaper. Most of the 10 to 15 correspondents sat together in a separate newsroom section, which did not have the same hierarchical structure as the other sections; others sat in the newsroom section that dealt with their thematic specialty.

There were also technicians and graphic assistants in the Newsroom. At the top of their pyramid was the art director, to whom graphic designers and graphic assistants reported. Graphic assistants were more numerous than graphic designers and took care of all the nonverbal elements of the newspaper, from tables and figures to charts, photographs, and page designs; designers had an overarching aesthetic responsibility in their section. Some of the graphic designers sat in the central office with the art director; others sat in "islands", next to the section with which they work most closely, separated by a wall. They sat in groups according to the visual elements of the newspaper they dealt with, and their division of tasks was specified in union agreements.

Only in the online newsroom did the graphic assistants sit in the same room as the journalists, although they were grouped in two different parts of the room. They inserted the headings, searched for pictures available for online publications in the databanks to which the newspaper subscribed, and prepared them for publication. They also prepared articles, videos, and webpages for publication, which meant that they inserted summaries, headings, and texts in the right places in the content management system. They were responsible for the homepage and the thematic pages. Of all the journalists, only the desk journalists and the editor had access to these functions.

Union agreements demanded a strict division of labor between journalists and graphic assistants. Even if the journalists could easily write their own headings or insert their pictures, they did not do it, because the job was restricted to graphic assistants. This division of labor between journalists and graphic assistants was a leftover from the original computerization of newspaper production. In fact, the introduction of the electronic editorial system in the 1980s was accompanied by significant organizational changes (Engwall, 1978; Smith, 1980). Many of the graphic technicians' tasks became obsolete, their job descriptions had to be changed, and the journalists had to learn to work with computers and an electronic content management system.

There are also four caretakers in the newsroom. Three of them sat on the third floor behind their desks in the common space between newsroom sections. The fourth sat on the second floor, where, as one of the journalists tells me, he has his kingdom, with a desk, pictures, and little religious icons around his corner. One of the caretakers' tasks is to distribute the mail and the newspaper copies in each section of the Newsroom, according to the individual needs of the journalists.

The Newsroom's organizational structure is inscribed in the products. The division of the newspaper into sections objectifies the Newsroom structure, any change in which can be traced from a change in the structure of the product. When a new supplement is created, for example, a new Newsroom section is likely created. Furthermore, in the middle of the newspaper, a table called the drum (*tamburo*) is published daily with the names of the top editors working in *Il Sole-24 Ore* Newsroom, including those whose products were not published that day. The bylines of the articles also leave a visible trace of who has performed the task of writing it and where that person is located.

ORGANIZING DAILY WORK IN THE NEWSROOM

In this section, I describe a typical day in the Newsroom, on the basis of the fieldnotes from the 110 days I spent there. This account is necessarily brief and omits many details. Its purpose is to provide the reader with a picture of everyday routines and activities, in order to contextualize the episodes that are described later. The two critical moments of the day are the morning and afternoon editorial meetings.

08:00–11:00 AM

There is hardly anyone in the Newsroom before 10:00 AM, except in the Online Newsroom. Some meetings in some Newsroom sections are planned for 09:00 or 09:30 AM, but they are usually dedicated to such specific issues as the contents of special sections or special pages or reportages, before starting the newswork of the day. Otherwise, the leading team of a section— ts Head Editor, Vice-Head Editor, and one or two of the Desk Editorse— omes to the Newsroom around 10:00 AM.

By 10:00 AM, the caretakers have brought copies of *Il Sole-24 Ore* and other newspapers of the day. The selection of newspapers to be delivered differs by section and is decided upon by the section's head editor. The newspaper copies come to the Newsroom with a piece of paper on top, indicating the number of copies delivered. All journalists take their own copies of the newspapers as they enter the roomus ually *Il Sole*, *La Repubblica*, and *Il Corriere*.

Sitting at their desks, they switch on their computers, check their e-mails, and check the newswires from the news agencies. They also check the websites of their main competitors, particularly *La Repubblica* and *Il Corriere*; they do not usually check *Il Sole-24 Ore*. They flip through the newspapers and check the news, how each item has been fitted onto the page, and how they have been dealt with. They compare *Il Sole-24 Ore*, particularly their own section, with the other newspapers to discover if they have missed something, often commenting aloud on the content of the other newspapers.

Before the editorial meeting begins, the head editors must prepare a list of news items that will be worked on that day and appear in the next day's newspaper. Some of these items come from the newswires, which gives them an idea of the top news of the day. Other items comprise pieces or packages of several articles from the section's archives. There are also weekly thematic pages, the contents of which have been planned during the entire week. To prepare the list of news of the day, each head or vice head editor also calls the correspondents— in Italy or abroad, depending on the section— o check if they have any urgent items.

Before the editorial meeting, the section's leading team starts distributing tasks to correspondents and freelancers, telling them to follow a certain issue and write a certain number of lines about them.

Mornings start earlier in the online newsroom. All the online staff rotates in two shifts. At the beginning of my study, these shifts were from 8:00 AM to 4:00 PM and from 11:00 AM to 7:00 PM, but later, after a new union agreement had been reached, the working hours of the online newsroom were extended from two overlapping 8-hour shifts encompassing 7:00 AM to 10:00 PM on weekdays and from 9:00 AM to 8:00 PM on weekends.

When the first journalists and graphic assistants (some 12 to 13 people) arrive, nobody else is in the Newsroom. The caretakers have not yet arrived, and sometimes even the newspapers of the day—*Il Sole-24 Ore*, *Il Corriere*, *La Repubblica* and *La Stampa*— ay not have arrived by 8:00 AM. When this happens, the journalists go to the reception desk to ask for them. Sometimes, the online newsroom receives the newspapers as late as 9:00 AM.

Work in the online newsroom consists primarily of a continuous checking of the newswire, an updating of news, or the creation of news to position on the website. The webpages may have different templates with different positions for the news, but the pagination does not need to be designed. In the first part of the morning, the desk editors look at the newspaper and select the articles that will be uploaded online. Editors usually tear out the pages containing those articles, and the respective pieces of paper are given to the graphic assistants, so they can find the articles in the newspaper's content management system. One of the desk journalists or the senior journalists or both select the articles, mark them with a pen, and give the newspaper to one or two graphic assistants, who enter the newspaper's editorial system and copy and paste the articles in the online editorial system. Then they format them properly, usually change the title according to the reporter's suggestion, and publish them by clicking the "publish" option in the content management system.

Not only articles are republished online; tables and graphs are also published. One of the reporters helps the graphic assistants to transfer tables and
graphs from the newspaper system to the online system. It is not always possible to transfer them directly, so the graphic assistants must sometimes take the
table from the newspaper and redesign it in the online system.

One of the desk editors is in charge of organizing the news of the day around
main topics and sending e-mails to the journalists in the online section, telling
them what they should follow and what pieces they should prepare, "so that
everybody does something; and by 9:00 AM we have some things to put in",
as one person told me.

The opening[8] or biggest headline of the website often replicates the opening
of the newspaper, but not necessarily. As the following short conversation
illustrates, the website editorial team may also choose a leading piece of news
that differs from that of the newspaper. The online editorial team can disagree
with the news hierarchy that has shaped the newspaper's front page and opt for
another piece of news for the homepage opening.

Besides selecting the paper articles that need to be uploaded online, the
journalists continuously check the news agency wire, in order to stay updated
on the development of the news.

Just as the priority of a news item changes during the course of the morning,
the desk editors change their opening and the position of the news on the
homepage. An opening can end up being a second or third headline, a new
piece of news can be entered, or a second or third headline can attain a higher
position on the homepage. This operation of changing the homepage is called
turning.

The reporters and desk editors often communicate with each other while
sitting at their desks, and necessarily raise their voices in order to do so. They
also shout to the graphic assistants, although they more freqe ntly go to the
assistants' desks because they need to explain things in detail. They often raise
their voices, and everyone within earshot is privy to their conversations and
their organizing work. They spend the majority of their time in front of the
computer, however, checking the news agency wires, the Internet and e-mail,
or writing their pieces. They always look busy; they often answer each other
(or me when I was there) while looking at the computer screen and are not
inclined to take time off for conversation, or even for a coffee at the bar.

The online journalists collaborate systematically with the foreign correspondents for qi ck pieces to be published online. And sometimes they col-

---

[8]   As explained in greater detail later, the opening is the biggest headline of the
page, which appears as the first headline on the homepage of the website or on the front
page of the newspaper.

laborate with newspaper journalists, with the help of the newspaperw ebsite coordinator, an editor who walks around the Newsroom and works as an intermediary between the online newsroom and the rest of the Newsroom.

11:00 AM–12:00 noon: Morning Editorial Meeting

On the second floor, in the middle of the Newsroom, is an enormous table surrounded by glass walls. This is the new editorial meeting room in the new building. During the first two weeks of my fieldwork, the editorial meeting was held there. Architect Renzo Piano had imagined this area to be:

> The heart of the Newsroom: There will be a big table where the editor-in-chief and the head editors will meet to choose the most important news of the day. ().. This will be a beautiful newsroom, transparent and open to participation. Journalists will have to feel at home there: Each one is at ease, discussing and sharing with others. They are all together: the editor-in-chief and every last one of the journalists. (Maugeri, 2003, pp. 30-31)

Piano's idea was clearly that the interior design, informed by a philosophy of openness and transparency, would shape the way of working. Renaissance architecture of Florence and its courts were the apparent source of inspiration for the space between the second and third floors. In the middle of the third floor is a big hole in the ceiling with a railing around it, so it is possible to look down from the third floor to the central part of the second floor, where Piano thought the large editorial table should be placed for editorial meetings.

Traditionally, this space was full of furniture and archival documents, and as the journalists told me, they had just tried to convert it into a useable meeting room when I arrived. At the time I was there, the glass room on the second floor had a table in the middle and three screens on the walls. The room was used only for meetings and only for two weeks, as the glass walls made for extremely poor acoustics. The meetings were then transferred to the old (and invisible) meeting room. I have learnt that the meetings were moved back to the glass room after I left, as work had been done to improve the acoustics.

The largest editorial meeting was held in the morning. There are about 20 participants daily, occupying the following positions:

- Editor-in-chief (1)
- Vice-chief editors[9] (3)

---

[9]   In the field stories narrated in this chapter, I use the term "chief editors" to refer to the leading editorial team of the newsroom, including the editor-in-chief and the vice-chief editors. This choice of terms helps me to maintain the anonymity of my interlocutors.

- The head editor of each newsroom section producing daily newspaper pages (5)
- The head editor of the newsroom section producing the next day's supplement (1 each day)
- Online editor (1)
- Central office editors (2 or 3 each day)
- Newsroom secretary (1)
- Newspaperw ebsite coordinator (1)
- Reporters (2 or 3)
- Coordinator of economic analysis (1)

The participants appeared to have some fixed seats. The editor-in-chief sat in the middle of one long side of the table in a seat implicitly reserved for him, with the vice-chief editors beside him. Even if the editor-in-chief is the last person to enter the meeting room, his seat remains unoccupied. If one of the vice-chief editors takes this place, it means that the editor-in-chief will be absent. If one of the section head editors is missing, a vice will serve as a substitute, and if no vice editor is present, one of the desk editors will replace the vice. The only positions that do not have a substitute are the newspaper–website coordinator and newsroom secretary, the latter having no voice in the meeting in any case.

The morning editorial meeting usually lasts from about 11:00 AM to 12:00 noon. All participants are physically present in Milan, except for the Roman head editor, who is in a teleconference from Rome, and whose vice editor participates in the meeting as well.

Before the meeting begins, the table is made ready, and the day's copies of the newspaper are distributed around the table. There is one copy for each seat available around the table, no matter how many people participate in the meeting. Newspaper copies are being opened as the chair of the meeting (the editor-in-chief or a vice-chief editor) comments upon the newspaper making the routine evaluation.

The day's online report is distributed by the online head editor, when present; it constitutes a sheet of paper with tables containing numbers of access to the website of the previous day and the homepage headings of the day's main competitors. Some head editors occasionally examine it, and the chair of the meeting may make explicit comments on this report. Presenting and commenting on the online report is not part of the automatic routines of the editorial meeting, however.

Head editors come to the meeting with handwritten notes about their section news menus. They take notes about the news menus of the other sections only if those sections are of particular interest. The online head editor takes extensive notes about all the other sections, will consider all the news menus when composing the website, and will also report the course of the meeting in full to the online news section.

The chief editors often come with some Post-it notes and remove them from a jacket pocket.

After the editorial meeting, most of the online report copies and the newspaper copies are left on the table.

The editor-in-chief talks mainly to the vice-chief editors, and listens when each section's head editor speaks in turn. They present the day's news menu, as if it were a shopping listt— heir expression. Each head editor addresses only the chief editors, and rarely jumps in when another editor is talking. People interrupt only to say that they have also worked on that topic or that they have some investigation on precisely that topic. It is as if head editors have a specific territory for which they are sole proprietor and sole ruler. Nobody except the chief editors, are entitled to enter this territory by giving feedback.

The head editors always speak in the same seqe nce and respect each other's turn. This all happens automatically; the editor-in-chief does not need to call upon each head editor to speak. The editorial meeting is highly structured:

Phase 1: Assessment
- One of the vice-chief editors evaluates the day's newspaper.
- The editor-in-chief comments on the website results, looking after the daily online results report. This does not happen often; nor does it have a consistent formula.

Phase 2: News "shopping list":
- Politics from the Roman newsroom
- Finance
- Italian economy
- Tax and law
- Foreign affairs
- Other issues (such as World and Markets, on Mondays)
- Commentaries and reportage

Phase 3: Closure

During the editorial meetings, the sign to begin is given by editor-in-chief's arrival and "Good morning". Often arriving some minutes late, the editor-in-chief sits between two vice-chief editors and sometimes, early in the discussion, mentions issues that could have been presented in another way in the newspaper or that have not been treated correctly. The floor is then turned over to one of the vice-chief editors in charge of the daily evaluation of the newspaper. Although nobody else intervenes in this evaluation unless called upon, it is understood that the chief editors are free to interrupt. After the assessment of the day's newspaper, each head editor presents the list of news of the day.

12:00 noon–2:00 PM

After the morning meeting, one of the central office editors writes a report containing the main news for each section and sends it to the head editors. Central office editors also negotiate with the advertising department about the space to be devoted to advertisements and then distribute a table to the head editors showing how the advertising space will be allocated on each page of the newspaper. They have an internal system to measure the dimension of articles and advertisements on the page; each is measured in *modules*, into which the page is divided. The proportion of journalistic advertising content changes throughout the day, and usually 3 or 4 different versions are sent to the sections from the central office until around 8:00 PM. Each time the space for advertisements changes, the pages need to be redesigned.

Most of the journalists working for a daily section of the newspaper arrive between 12:00 noon and 1:00 PM, so they can listen to the debriefing about the morning editorial meeting that their head editor delivers around that time. The head editors perform this task in different ways, but most of them concentrate only on their own thematic area, telling their section the topics of the day that have been presented in the meeting and how they are assigned among the journalists. After the section meeting, head editors, together with their vice-editors, start designing the pages on paper according to the advertisement information received from the central office. Once a first draft of the pages is ready and the assignment distributed in the newsroom around 2:00 PM, it is time for lunch.

In the online newsroom, work continues in an uninterrupted flow until lunch time: checking the wires, updating the website, and preparing special pages. When the online editor returns from the editorial meeting and becomes part of the flow, work continues as usual. Half an hour or so after the meeting, the other journalists gather around the online editor's desk for a debriefing about the editorial meeting. This is a good moment to plan collaboration with newspaper journalists and coordination within the online newsroom.

2:00–2:30 PM: lunch

2:30–3:00 PM

When they return from lunch, coffee, and cigarettes, it is time to check the newswires and redesign the pages. Then the head editors go to the afternoon editorial meeting, while the remaining editors start thinking about their pieces and go to the polygraphers to give them the hand-designed pages (on paper), which the polygraphers redesign on Hermes, the content management software. This activity is called pagination, and Hermes stores both news from the news agency and articles from published issues of the newspaper. Thus, the polygraphers take the pages that the editors have designed on paper and reproduce them on Hermes.

All day, every day, negotiations on the positioning of advertising in the next day's newspaper continue between the Newsroom and the advertising sales department in Business. Throughout the day, the central office (different editors in charge of the central office) sends the Newsroom personnel different versions of the so-called *foliazione*, a pagination scheme that is circulated both in print and via e-mail in the Newsroom. This distribution changes over time, because it is the result of an ongoing negotiation between the changing needs and reqe sts of the news on the one hand and the changing needs and reqe sts of the advertisers on the other hand. The advertising sales managers have usually sold certain positions in the newspaper to their clients already, but these positions can be filled only in accordance with the space needed for the day's news. Throughout the day, the initial distribution of advertising space that accommodated the reqe sts of the advertisers may change because of reqe sts from various editors or from central office. A specialized advertising manager and one editor in the central office negotiate, primarily via e-mail and phone, and rarely by visiting the advertising person in the Newsroom's central office. All the other editors receive the pagination several times a day and act accordingly.

The pagination comprises five columns. The first column to the left indicates the page number, the second indicates the section of the newspaper, and the three remaining columns to the right indicate the dimension of the advertisement space and the advertiser.

The editors of the various sections use the pagination to design their pages by hand. They have templates for designing the entire section, but they rarely use them. In fact, I have seen these schemes used only for the newspaper technology supplement *Nova*. None of the other editors were designing their section with the help of such templates, and in the finance section the head editor and the head editor's desk team design even the overall structure of its section, which is a separate supplement distributed four days a week.

Each single page is then designed on paper, a process that begins by marking out the advertisement space. Often, but not always, the editors use a pre-structured sheet divided into small sqa res that represent the units of measurement of the space for advertising content. The space for journalistic content is divided in rows, and the editors know the approximate conversion rate between sqa res and rows.

The pages designed on paper are then copied into the computer. The editors give their paper designs to the polygraphers, who begin by marking with a diagonal line the space needed for the advertisements, which appear on their screens and those of the journalists. This space is inaccessible to the Newsroom.

Once the electronic page is designed, the journalists can access its various journalistic spaces and write their pieces in them. The advertising department is in charge of uploading the advertisements in the system.

From Hermes, the journalists can print the pages of the newspaper as they will appear in the final product, which they do several times a day at several stages of the work. When they close their pages, they print the final version and bring it to the central office, so the central office editors and one of the vice-chief editors can check the entire newspaper. This process of printing and delivering a printed copy to the central office constitutes *closure*.

5:00–5:30 PM: Afternoon Editorial Meeting

The afternoon editorial meeting takes place at 5:00 PM in the same room as the morning meeting. Head editors from each section, central office editors, the chief editors, and the art director participate. This meeting, aimed at designing the front page of the newspaper, is organized in three phases:

- Phase 1: Led by the editor-in-chief, a discussion can be opened by any editor to make general comments on the news of the day.
- Phase 2: All head editors of a section present the news that they consider as having enough potential newsworthiness to allow it to be promoted on the front page.
- Phase 3: The editor-in-chief, sitting next to the art director, proposes the design for the front page, which the art director sketches on paper. The editor-in-chief discusses this with the vice-chief editors and some of the interested editors.

5:30–8:00 PM

After the meeting, head editors debrief their journalists in their own section—particularly their vice and desk editorsa— bout the design of the homepage, and thus the small pieces that will be eventually reqi red for the front page. Then it is time for the journalists to write and for the editors to check how the pages are coming along. Between 7:00 and 9:00 PM, the Newsroom is silent of human voices, but clamorous with the noise of machines.

After dinner, work in the online newsroom continues as usual. The journalists take their lunch break in shifts, so the website is never *uncovered*, as they say. The online head editor goes to the afternoon editorial meeting, and when he returns, puts himself back into the flow again. The afternoon editorial meeting does not provide crucial insights into the online work, because it is mainly about the front page.

Later in the afternoon, some of the desk editors write the online news promotions that are placed in the newspaper on the second or fourth page.

At 8:00 PM, the online newsroom closes. Journalists and graphic assistants leave. Often, however, due to the development of news, some of the journalists and graphic assistants stay later, to keep the website updated.

8:00–9:00PM: Until the Closure of the Newspaper Pages

Around 9:30 PM, the pages should close and be delivered to the central office, where editors check them. When the pages are delivered in print from Hermes to the central office and the paper has been put together, the central office editors of the night shift and one vice-chief editor read all the pages, with particular emphasis on headlines, infographics, and the use of pictures. They also revise the work of their colleagues, so there are no repetitions, and the news is updated according to the latest news agency takesa— process called *approving the pages*. They have until midnight to close the newspaper and send it online to the printing plants, where the first edition is printed. Shortly after midnight, the first edition is delivered online to the Newsroom, where the vice-chief editor and one of the central office editors check it and make any necessary changes for the second edition. At 2:00 AM the next day, the second edition is printed. Although the first edition is printed and distributed nationally, the second edition is printed and distributed only in Milan and Rome and therefore differs slightly from the edition sold in other regions of the country.

TESTING, NEGOTIATING, AND COMPROMISING: FOUR CRITICAL MOMENTS

It is considered crucial for the autonomy of journalism to maintain a separation between journalism and management, between the Newsroom and the Business, and therefore necessary to watch for any attempts at influencing journalistic content, and thus ultimately endangering the independent press (Raviola, 2014). As Alex said in his lecture:

> If there were a perfect separation between the two sides of the organization, I would not even need to mention this. But we live nowadays in very imperfect times, when the ownerst— hrough managersof ten try to influence the activities of the editorial department. (Bocconi University, Milan, September 2007)

The contacts between the Newsroom and the Business sometimes result in open conflict over the scarcity of resources or the interference of managers, advertisers, and shareholders in journalistic work. At *Il Sole-24 Ore*, the organizational separation between the Newsroom's journalism and the Company's management framed the practical arrangements of a compromise. The mutual recognition of this separation̶ ournalists do journalism and managers manage̶ ramed the encounters between employees as negotiations between journalism and management. The organizational separation was considered vital to the independence of journalism from the owners and from advertising, managerial control, and marketing.

The following sections of this chapter focus on four critical moments, during which the organizational separation has been contested, breached, and sometimes established anew. All these critical moments concerned journalism–advertising negotiations in various forms and in relation to various products.

About Supplements: Reconquering the Periphery of the Newspaper

The daily newspaper that is printed, distributed, eventually sold, and hopefully read, is a composite object incorporating the compromise between news and money as principles of value for news organizations. Literally every day and all day long, the amount and position of advertisements in a daily newspaper are being negotiated between the advertising department and the relevant newsroom editor. Although the distinction between journalistic and advertising contents should be clearly inscribed on each page of the newspaper, there are times when journalists or advertisers do not see this inscription as satisfying. In such cases, the two principles of value may be tested against each other, and a new compromise may be reached and inscribed anew in new products.

One such instance was the practice of sponsored pages, which started at the newspaper in 2000, after the dot.com bubble burst, and advertising revenue decreased. At the time of my study, it was a relatively freqe nt practice to have two, four, or even six pages of the newspaper filled with content written by journalists and looking like journalistic content but sponsored by advertisers. The words "advertising information" or "sponsored pages" on top of each of these pages indicated to the reader that this was not journalistic content.

As the newspaper is a composite object, some parts have become more vulnerable than others to confusion between journalistic writing and advertising content. One of the most-qe stioned newspaper products was the thematic supplement, the *Rapporti*. When sponsored pages were first published, the Business section of the organization decided to dismantle the journalistic team responsible for producing thematic supplements and transform them in advertising pages "with an advertising information content". As Charlie, one of the editors, told me:

> [The fact that the supplements around 2002 did not have a dedicated journalistic team] has generated a lot of problems, because it's clear that in the absence of a Newsroom defending journalistic practices, the advertising sellers went wild, like in the Wild West, and there was an assault on the Newsroom, in order to inform the journalists about this or that company that the advertising sellers had talked to. It's clear that the sellers sometimes bump into information about the advertisers that could be news, because when a company undertakes an advertising campaign, it wants to communicate something, usually because there's a change going on. At this point, there's usually also news. This doesn't change the fact that in our job, and in this newspaper, it's inappropriate for an advertising seller to call a journalist to say that there's news. (Interview with Charlie, September 2007)

It is not an exclusive right of the journalists to discover the news, therefore; rather it is because of respect for the institutional distinction between journalistic and business reqi rements that the identification and selection of the news must be the purview of the journalists. It is inappropriate for the advertising salespeople to cross the line. The text may not be a pure piece of news, but the people qa lified as journalists must be the ones to make that classification. If people from the Business side, like salespeople, begin associating themselves with that textby writing and designing it, for examplet— he text loses its journalistic qa lity and becomes advertising. In cases in which objects normally carry inscriptions of various possible classifications, their mobility and multiplicity may be particularly sensitive. That contamination must be avoided. Charlie continued:

> Such an event is experienced as contamination between information and advertising. Contamination occurs when the advertising agent serves as the intermediary between journalists and sources of information [like companies]. An advertising agent could also sell the journalistic content or just be misunderstood by a client that would expect a journalistic report on its own business. And there could be a *quid pro quo*: "As an advertising agent, I put you in contact with the Newsroom and you, as an advertiser, buy our advertising spaces." There is no proof that it has always been done this way, because the selling network has always been well briefed [to hide this practice] on this point. In any case, the advertising sellers are the wrong people to act as intermediaries. They must say to their company: "The news seems to be interesting; you need to call the Newsroom or send a press release, and they'll decide what to do." (Interview with Charlie, September 2007)

The contact between salespeople and journalists is best avoided because it could undermine the autonomy of journalists, add pressure to the newspaper's duty to inform citizens, and ultimately interfere in the independence of the press. As Charlie continued:

> Therefore, when there have been some episodes of advertising-selling agents who—even as a goodwill gesture— alled the Newsroom, or sometimes threatened… that if an article does not come out, they won't provide advertising, sometimes even with the rope around their necks, they called [to communicate] these conditions… This has created problems, which were reported in the assembly of journalists and were stigmatized by our union committee. (Interview with Charlie, September 2007)

Charlie claimed that it does not matter if the intentions behind certain actions are good or bad. They simply must not occur. Charlie made clear to me that it is the task of journalists to reaffirm the commitment to journalistic autonomy, by setting distinct and impermeable boundaries around the Newsroom. As Charlie told me at a later encounter, the advertising salespeople try to breach these boundaries: "It's their job." But Charlie sees one of an editor's functions as "an educational role with regard to the Business and the advertising sales agency, by fixing rules and checking that they're respected, on the basis of our duty code and our contract" (Fieldnotes, November 2007).

According to Charlie, the attempts by advertising salespeople to cross the boundaries are stronger when a journalist is a junior professional whose practices are still are not well inculcated, and who can possibly be bent to the will of the advertisers. The editor told me that when, at a certain point, the size of the supplements was doubled or tripled each week in order to please the advertising investors, the Newsroom secretary in charge of their coordination could not handle the situation any longer:

> So, the qa lity decreased, and the advertising and the Business had a more and more proactive role, which was experienced by the Newsroom as practically aggressive. The number of these supplements also increased. At this point, the editor-in-chief proposed that [name of an editor] become *Rapporti*'s head editor.

Apparently, the job was not easya— t least not at the beginning. Charlie tells of an episode that marked the shift between the supplement being the territory of advertising to its being reconqe red by journalism. Shortly after a new editor was assigned to the supplement, at the publication of one issue of the supplement, the position of an advertisement was changed without notifying the Newsroom. It turned out that in a supplement on the car industry, an advertisement for a car appeared adjacent to the page on which appeared an article about the same car presented at a fair. This problem of advertising and journalism juxtapositioned in the supplement was repeated several times in the supplementa— no-go move by the new editora— nd an apology came from the advertising sales department. As Charlie commented, "One can interpret [this episode] as a malicious act or as pure coincidence. Let's say that I believed their apologies. At any rate, such things don't happen any longer."

Other editors emphasized that a total lack of contact between the advertisers and the editorial staff must exist. As Andrea, an old-timer journalist, told me, the new supplement editor ensured that there was no direct link between the advertisers and the topic of the articles: "It is necessary to avoid even the slightest impression of collusion between advertising and the Newsroom, so that readers are certain that there is no possibility that such blending could occur" (Conversation with Andrea, September 2007).

It is no coincidence that this episode concerns a supplement rather than the main body of the newspaper. When I asked if the situation differed for online content, Charlie replied that online advertising was still relatively marginal, and that the bargaining power of selling agents in that medium was much lower. It is difficult for the newspaper to resist when an advertiser that wants a supplement to be created on a certain topic puts 250,000 EUR on the table. Charlie concluded: "It is difficult, but sometimes absolutely necessary. Even so, we must be friends, as before."

About Sponsoring Content: Concessions in the Main Spine of the Newspaper

The non-supplement parts of the newspaper were inscribed with new ways of reaching a compromise between journalistic and advertising content. Enter *quartoss*— upplements in a format obtained by folding a sheet of paper into four leaves. In this case of qa rtos, the pages are sponsored by advertisers and focus on a topic of interest to them. These pages look like regular newspaper pages, except for a small heading on top, signaling the fact that the pages are sponsored. The practice of using *quartos* began at the turn of the millennium, when the advertising market experienced a significant recession and newspapers needed to find new ways to gain revenue. Quartos were first published without a heading signaling that they were sponsored, but the heading was later inserted, and qa rtos became a common component of the newspaper.

One day, during the course of my study, two people from the advertising department visited one of the Newsroom sections. They wanted to talk about a qa rto on nuclear energy.

They said that they had agreed with the sponsor that there would be two half pages.

> Robin (advertising person): We have thought about focusing on ENEL, Edison, and
>   Ansaldo, because they have central sites in [City X].
> Avery, head editor of the section (to Jordan, vice-head editor): The e-mail you have
>   sent with the program of the section on nuclear energy. Can you send it to
>   Robin as well?
> Robin: Perfect! Thanks. So I will have a better idea.
> Avery: But we don't go beyond four pages.
> Robin: No, no.
> Avery: I know you, and you will have me making six.

After the advertising people left, Avery uttered: "Unbelievable! They do a collection of advertising money targeted to specific thematic pages." He rhetorically reinforced the exceptionality of this situation and the normal separation of journalism and advertising in deciding what is worthy of publication. This is a common practice in the news field, but evidently it could still raise indignant comments.

This short conversation demonstrates that the relationship between journalists and the advertising people is not as neat as the principles prescribe: Negotiations take place every day to reach compromises on how to inscribe both democracy and profitability in the newspaper. It is part of the daily work of journalists to keep the advertising managers and sales agents in their placebot h in the sense of their office space and in the sense of their attributed place in the newspapert— hereby making and remaking the separation between the Newsroom and Business, between management and journalism.

Concerns about the relationship between advertising and journalistic content also arise around the main body of the daily. Each day, the journalists writing for the daily receive a scheme or plan indicating the number of pages per section and the advertising space on each page. The design of the pages by the editors and their deputies begins with a design of the advertising spaces— pace that is lost to the journalists and to journalism. The pagination changes several times during the day, as the advertising people negotiate with advertisers and talks proceed between journalists in the Newsroom and the people paginating in the advertising department. Every time the scheme changesa— bout four or five times a dayt— he pages need to be redesigned, beginning with the placement of advertising space.

Desk editors and the online newsroom editors are responsible for designing the pages so as to avoid the products or brands being advertised in the same page, or even the page before or after an article about the company.

Not only is the advertising content discussed in relation to journalistic content, but the position of advertising is a matter of constant discussion

(Raviola, 2010; Raviola & Dubini, 2016). During one morning editorial meeting, a fascinating conversation ensued. On that day, the newspaper had a full-page advertisement on pages 9 and 11—on the odd-numbered pages that appear to the right when opening the newspaper. Those pages are believed to be the ones that receive the most attention by the readers, so advertisement prices for spaces on the odd-numbered, right-hand pages are appropriately higher. One of the editors was given the floor to start presenting the day's news menu:

> Parker (editor): Excuse me, maybe this is my obsession, but don't you get upset when you see the full advertising page to the right?
> Kyle (chief editor): Yes, but everybody does it that way.
> Quinn (another editor): Yeah, the women's magazines started it.
> Kyle: We are the ones that have given up to these tendencies the least [having full-page advertising on odd pages]. We have tried to keep a barrier.
> Hayden (chief editor): They have even asked to have the third page!
> Kyle: And we have said no to all the formats. The supplement on luxury goods is a tabloid, ok. But in the *Rapporti*, the journalists have regained the areas that had been, if I may say so, devastated by false journalists from advertising. We believe that the readers can distinguish between true journalism and advertising, though it is not so sure, as the press reviews show. At any rate, the two pages inside need to be revised.

Kyle was referring to two pages with "promotional content" created by the advertising department. In the day's newspaper, they were pages 28 and 29 in the Tax and Law section.

Placing a full-page advertisement represents a concession to economic pressures and a compromise reached by giving up journalistic space to commercial advertising, directly contributing to increased revenues. An odd-numbered page full of ads is highly visible to the readers, who have the ad in front of their eyes as big as the news, as they flip the pages to the left. As size and place have symbolic importance, this is a significant concession to economic pressure. Yet, the page with ads is still visibly distinct from those with the journalistic content.

A Thematic Website: Authoring as a Way of Classifying a Website

Realizing that newspapers and news websites are composite and multiple objects, and that their classification is neither straightforward nor self-evident, the established organizational practice in the independent press is to avoid contact between journalists and advertising people in their daily work. The assumption is that these are different jobs, driven by different interests, and reqi ring different mindsets. Conseqe ntly, the relationship between the Newsroom and Business (especially the advertising side of Business) must be kept as loose as possible. The very fact that this message was formulated so strongly by Alex in the university lecture mentioned in the above section on *Il Sole 24 Ore: a closer view*, suggested that it was under threat and needed constant reinforcement.

Another editor—Drewbe lieves that the relationship between advertising and journalistic content is more complex on the web than it is in the newspaper:

> You must identify the brand of cell phones or computers and take a position on them because the reader wants to know, but you must maintain journalistic honesty. When the managers have advertisers interested in a special topicf— ranchising, for examplet— hey ask if we intend to make a special issue. (Conversation with Drew, October 2007)

Drew supported special issues and co-marketing. When Nokia pays to make a service on cell phones, Drew argued, it is like a "technical sponsor"a— sponsor that promotes a cultural or sport event through the payment of goods and services necessary for that event.

> It's a delicate relationship, but the task of desk editors is to check that the content is newsworthy, and not just an interview with an important manager talking about his own products [to promote them]. (Conversation with Drew, October 2007)

Journalistic vs. non-journalistic: This is how products are classified at the newspaper. They are journalistica— nd therefore made in the service of democracyi— f journalists hired by *Il Sole-24 Ore* or other news organizations, like news agencies, have written them. They are non-journalistica— nd in this case made for profiti— f written by marketing people or salespeople or anyone else not employed as a journalist. This is eqa lly valid for the newspaper and the website. Certain websites are journalistic and written by employed journalists. Others are non-journalistic and written by marketing people or outsourced to external content providers. In this setting, as I noted elsewhere (Raviola & Norbäck, 2013), the qa lification of the author as a journalist can be used as a proof that the product, like a website or a single article, is journalistic.

Journalistic authorship is stressed in the union agreement signed for the onlinepa per-integration project, as implicitly opposed to managerial or marketing authorship: "The online newsroom keeps the original production of contents" (Union Agreement, 2007, p. 2). In the integration project, the content published online should be produced by journalists working in the online section of the Newsroom, and not by someone outside the Newsroom, as happened for some of the websites at the time the agreement was being negotiated. This specification was articulated in a multimedia union agreement that was circulated internally:

> The presence of the Il Sole-24 Ore Group website will increase with new projects that will see direct participation of journalists on the information side. All the vertical portals[10] on the web will have an adeqa te journalistic content ().. The new portals (for example *Job24* or *House24*) with information content will always have a journalist as a reference point/contact/responsible.
> Business will commit itself to favoring the new ways of working agreed upon with the Newsroom and to put in place adeqa te technologies in order to favor collaboration and development of new projects.

The first paragraph of this qot e focuses on the Newsroom journalists, whereas the second shifts attention to the Business (which, in journalistic language, means everybody outside the Newsroom) is in charge of providing technology and support to the integration project. Newsroom and Business are clearly separated here in two distinct paragraphs and given specific areas of responsibility.

The internal presentation of one of the thematic websites at its launch can well illustrate the emphasis given to the adjective "journalistic" in association with "online".

On a Friday morning in September 2007, the meeting room was filled with head editors and vice-chief editors sitting at their places, ready to start the news conference of the day. Skyler, the editor responsible for the new website entered, along with Finley and Frankie, two junior journalists working for the website. When Kyle arrived and opened the meeting, Skyler took the lead and started presenting the product of their work, while technicians were connecting the teleconference screen to the laptop. Finley and Frankie sat and listened to the presentation, barely lifting their eyes to look at the audience. They kept staring at the laptop screen in front of them.

The website comprises various sections, which Skyler listed. For the launch, the journalists and their editor focused on the design festival in London and asked some fashion designers to describe their own cities. The site would be updated on Mondays and Thursdays, Skyler said, except for the fashion weeks, when it would be updated daily. During the presentation, the editor repeated that the aesthetic and journalistic efforts were remarkable. Kyle added:

> The website has journalistic content *sensu stricto*. It is not an e-commerce website. Making this choice, we anticipated what others would do. (Fieldnotes, September 2007)

---

[10] Vertical portals are websites specializing in certain themes, such as luxury, jobs, or houses. Here I simply call them thematic websites.

The chief editor added that the website is journalistic in nature, as it was created and organized by a journalist, and also explained what the website *was not*: It was not an e-commerce website. As this statement was in anticipation of what the competitors would do, the statement about the e-commerce aspect implied that the other competitors' websites were not journalistic— erely e-commerce websites. In this way, Kyle reclaimed the new object within the journalistic space: The website itself, literally inscribed with articles written by journalists and designed in accordance with the judgment of journalists, became proof of the victory of journalistic principles over mere commercial interests.

Now Drew, a central desk editor, took the floor: "Some interactive spices are added— rticle evaluation and polls available to the readers." Although Kyle attempted to make the new object proof of traditional journalism, Drew emphasized new possibilities allowed by the website. For Drew, this object was a proof of a new journalism. The food metaphor (spices) seemed to suggest the complementarity of these new possibilities— ike evaluating articles and making readers' polls— o the core journalistic character of the website. Interactivity is thus like a spice to the main journalistic fare.

Before closing the presentation, Skyler added that there were still some technical problems related to the homepage, but before Monday "there was an ocean of time to go" and "the homepage, just like the front page of the newspaper, was the last one to close" (Fieldnotes, September 2007). At the end, Kyle, alluding to but not looking at Finley and Frankie, said: "They were interns, and they made this project. These young colleagues have come with a project in hand. And here it is, made real."

The public presentation of the new thematic website became an opportunity to reclaim the new digital object into the journalistic space, although adding possible ways to realize journalistic principles. The website was defined as journalistic, even journalistic *sensu stricto*, ultimately marking a victory of democracy over profit as a principle of worth. In proving this victory, the analogy with the newspaper and its production process served as a manifestation of the journalistic worth of the website: regular updates like those in the weekly sections of the newspaper, clear distance from e-commerce, and treatment of the homepage like the front page contributed to making the website's "journalistic *sensu stricto*". The new interaction possibilities of the website are just spices, not a proof of journalistic value.

About Promotion on the Main Website: Defending or Threatening Journalism

The following story concerns a thematic website and the main news website (see also Raviola & Norbäck, 2013; Raviola & Dubini, 2016). It relates to the coordination between Oakley and Denver, junior journalists working for the thematic website; and Jael and Brighton, senior online journalists.

It was the end of September 2007, and because of events taking place in Milan, it was a busy morning for Oakley and Denver. They were hanging around the city with their editor in their branded Smart Car, carrying their branded microphones for interviews and videos. They had to follow events in the city, then return to the Newsroom to write and to ask the personnel in the press offices of the event organizers to send photos for their website photo galleries. The air was filled with tension and adrenaline. It was the first acid test for the team since the launch of the website.

Late one Tuesday morning, the thematic website team had organized a live-stream transmission of one of the happenings. The thematic website editor was at the happening, ready to go online live. Oakley was behind the desk in the Newsroom in direct mobile connection with the editor. Denver was at another show, which was to be reported on later that day. The rest of the online newsroom was following the daily news flow.

As was the custom since the beginning of website operations, Jael, the senior journalist, introduced live streaming on the main news website home-page in the morning. After a couple of hours, when the streaming was about to start, Brighton, a senior colleague of Jael's, noticed that the announcement had disappeared from the main website homepage and encouraged Oakley, a junior journalist, to post the announcement on the ilsole24ore.com homepage. Oakley had already noticed the announcement had been on the homepage and had disappeared.

The website still had the old design layout, with a section in salmon pink (for the main website news), a section in white (for links to other thematic portals connected to the main website), and a section in light blue (for promo-tional content), organized in compartments called *boxes*. The light blue boxes were to be used only by the marketing department as promotional space for *Il Sole-24 Ore* products. As Brighton suggested, Oakley used the light blue boxes on the main news homepagea— fter further encouragement from another journalist and with the technical support of the graphic assistants. Oakley had never inserted anything in those boxes before, and misplacing a piece of text in the wrong box would create confusion for readers and journalists as to what was news and what was advertising. Publishing a piece of news in a light blue box, for example, would mislead readers and other journalists to think that that item was promotional content rather than news.

The live streaming started, and the announcement was on the homepage in one of the light blue boxes. Oakley was excited about this first live streaming and shared the excitement with the thematic website editor through an almost continuous mobile connection. At this point, Jael, who had first put the announcement on the homepage in the early morning, came closer to Oakley's desk:

> Let me ask you a qe stion out of curiosity. You have to answer me clearly. If this website enters the advertising spacea— nd I'm not saying this for nothingI— won't write even one single line about it anymore. If that's advertising, none of it will enter the news space. It's incredible! I put a post on the homepage, and I find that the news turned into advertising after two hours! At this point, nobody even had the decency to tell me…

On the defensive from Jael's attack, Oakley said that it was Brighton who had reqe sted that the link be moved into the light blue boxes. And the discussion continued:

> Jael: I'm not picking on you. You're a junior without responsibility. I'm in charge of managing the journalistic part. If it stays there, it doesn't go anywhere else.

Jael calms down and speaks in a calmer tone of voice.

> Jael: These doubts have existed since the birth of journalism. No problem.

But Jael is still visibly irritated.

> Jael: If it's an advertisement, we've solved a problem. If it's advertising, it isn't journalism any longer. At least here there is not even the hypocrisy any longer. My role is to take care of journalism!

The discussion was interrupted by other news that needed to be updated. About a half hour later, reported the episode to Denver, the other junior journalist working for the thematic website. Behind their desks, in front of their computers, without their eyes leaving the screen, they started discussing what happened.

> Oakley: At one point, the image is gone. The photo news on the homepage, I mean. It is not there any longer. So, I asked Brighton: "Excuse me. They have taken it away without telling me anything. Where should I put it?" I was told to use the box in light blue.
> Denver: Oh no! Not that one!
> Oakley (reacting promptly): Well, I put it there. Then, Jael sees it and…

Denver interrupted the story and started talking about the other happening. It ended with somebody in a wedding dress with water scenery in the backgroundve ry scenic, Denver thought. Then the focus returned to the episode, and Oakley continued to justify the way it went down:

> Oakley: I talked to the boss before doing anything. And then, Jael says, "I won't take care of it any longer if it stays there."
> Denver: And Jael is right.
> Oakley: But what could I do? They didn't have space. Brighton told me to put it there. And I did.
> Denver: You don't have to rely on such a senior journalist.
> Oakley: Then the portal editor should talk to the boss. They decide. I just want to do a good job.
> Denver: I understand, but we have to fight for this website. Has Jael attacked you? It was already clarified. The boxes must be used when there is no news for the thematic websiteonl y for promotion of the website.

Denver mentioned an established rulet— hat the promotional box had to be used exclusively to make the thematic website more visible as a website, but not to promote certain news. Otherwise, the news is interpreted as advertising.

Brighton, who had suggested putting the announcement of the live streaming in the light blue box, returned later in the afternoon, saw that the announcement was still on the homepage, and warned the junior journalists:

> Brighton: See to it that you take away that live streaming from the homepage of the website. If you take charge of something, you must follow it.
> Denver: Ok, but may I say something? We use the light blue box only when there is no news [when the insert is merely promotional; anything placed in a light blue box is interpreted as advertising].
> Brighton (unaware of the heated episode): Put it wherever they like. I made this suggestion just because from there [the light blue boxes] it's possible to put a direct link to the website.

Whatever was written in the white and salmon pink boxes of the website could not be linked to another website directly; it would first link to a short article within the website, and a link to another website could be included in that short article. The reader then clicked on a title on the homepage, and a webpage with some lines of text opened, allowing the reader to find the link and click on it.

The priorities behind the decisions of the two senior journalists were obviously different. The usability of the website, the facility with which it can be accessed, and the importance of maximizing the clicks, were all of greater interest to Brighton than was any visual distinction between journalistic and advertising space. Both sets of practicesm aking the website accessible and distinguishing it from advertisingw ere considered of journalistic worth, but the light blue boxes constituted a material artifacte— omprised a concrete space of controversy. This episode illustrates the ambiguity of the new objectt— he websitebe tween old and new journalistic practices, and the experienced newspaper practitioner's attempts to clear a purely journalistic space and eliminate a controversial space by setting the supremacy of one set of practices over another one.

Another interesting aspect of this story is the way in which Oakley went into defense mode against Jael's accusations by saying that it was Brighton, another senior journalist, who suggested the use of the light blue space. In this way, Oakley evoked another of the journalism norms:

> Responsibility of the journalist.
> ().. The journalist accepts indications and directives only from the journalistic hierarchies of his own newspaper, as long as these dispositions are not contrary to the professional law, to the national contract and to the Charter of Duties. (*Ordine dei Giornalisti*, The Charter of Journalists' Duties, 1993, p. 2)

In other words, Oakley defended the violation of the journalistic principle of autonomy (through separation of journalistic and advertising content) by evoking another professional principle (accepting directives from journalistic hierarchies). This, in fact, had the effect of dissipating the conflict, perhaps by reminding the old-timers of the difficulty of reconciling different principles of worth.

When the website design was renewed, the distinction between salmon pink and light blue backgrounds disappeared, no longer signaling the distinction between journalistic and advertising content, which created some irritation in the online newsroom. One of the desk journalists claimed several times in talking to the editors that the distinction between advertising and journalistic content no longer existed as a design feature. The desk journalist believed that this blending created confusion, as it broke the established and visible alignment between author and place, which had once signaled the distinction between journalistic and advertising/promotional (business-like) content. A multimedia marketing manager responded that these were internal issues that should not be reflected on the website, finally declaring the victory of marketing thinking over the controversial space that Jael had tried to make journalistically pure.

DISCUSSION: MULTIPLICITY OF THE OBJECT AND ITS QUALIFICATIONS

Although previous scholars have discussed how the separation between journalism and management has been transformed and transgressed in web-related projects (e.g., Fagerling & Norbäck, 2005), my analysis demonstrates how the established organizational compromise of separation between Newsroom and Business is more fragile and contested than is usually acknowledged.

The relationship between journalism and management at *Il Sole-24 Ore* was established as a separation between two parts of the company—ewsroom and Business—hat continued to evolve (Raviola, 2010, 2014; Raviola & Norbäck, 2013). This way of organizing independence was the closest I came to theories and stories I had encountered in media studies: that of a Chinese Wall and of a strong defense of the Newsroom vis-à-vis Business.

This way of organizing implied that journalism was represented and performed exclusively by journalists, whereas management was exclusively performed by business people. My stories from the field study in the Italian financial newspaper provided hints at the everyday and not-so-everyday negotiations between Newsroom and Business, mainly through a handful of people who were working at the boundaries between the two parts of the company or sometimes crossed the boundaries to the other side. From the analyses of tests, negotiations, and compromises presented in this chapter, I conclude by identifying two of the specific learnings I have gleaned from this case: the fluidity of the website and the correspondence between action and occupation.

One of the first things I learned was that the digital space—*the website—was treated as a more fluid object of work than the print newspaper was,* in relation to the inscription of the separation between journalism and management. But gray zones of negotiation between the two were not exclusive to the making of the website (see also Raviola & Dubini, 2016). From the perspective of the Newsroom, drama and defensive language emphasized the high stakes involved in journalism in the service of democracy—xhibited both in an advertisement placed on an odd page of the newspaper and in a journalist's text misplaced on the website. It was these acts of defense that made the Newsroom "pure" (Raviola, 2014), and they were often triggered by traces of invasion left on news products.

I also learned about *the correspondence between practices and occupational communities,* that they could be used both as a proof of the danger to journalistic autonomy and as a proof of the restoration of this very autonomy. Journalists reclaiming the space of a supplement that had been controlled by the advertising department made that very supplement journalistic—s much as journalists misplacing a text in promotional website space reserved for business people were endangering journalism. The author of a certain action and the object of work are used to qa lify the very action as journalistic or managerial.

As I mentioned, the study presented in this chapter is the closest I came to what I considered the traditional way of organizing independence in established newspapers. Against the background of increasingly contested practices, like blogging, introduced by outsiders to the journalistic community, and of new activities to counteract the economic crisis of newspapers, I was left wondering how independence was organized in other contexts and how that organization would look if I had been sitting some place other than the traditional Newsroom.

3. Independence through expansion: making news for profit

A concentration of ownership has increased in the news industry over the past decade (Noam, 2016) as larger newspapers or media organizations have acqi red smaller news publications, creating changes in competition. Japanese publisher Nikkei acqi red the *Financial Times* from Pearson in 2015. The so-called trio BNP—Pierre Bergé, Xavier Niel, and Mathieu Pigasse, who owned the iconic French newspaper *Le Monde* bought *Le Nouvel Observateur* magazine in 2013.[1] In many European countries, larger groups, often concentrating media ownership into a few larger companies, have acqi red local newspapers. Newspapers that have mastered the creation of qa lity content have recently been objects of interest for large tech companies that have mastered the digital economy. Jeff Bezos, founder of Amazon, bought *The Washington Post* in 2013, and Marc and Lynne Beioff from the tech company Salesforce bought *Time Magazine* in 2018, to mention but a few examples. The acqi sitions of news organizations show a global trend in valuing news organizations in economic terms rather than seeing them "as organs of opinion-formation or party platforms, as was once the case" (Hadenius & Weibull, 1999, p. 144).

The issue of media ownership concentration has caught the attention of policy makers and non-governmental organizations internationally, mainly in connection with the relationship between ownership and the freedom of journalists. Although some commentators estimate that that concentration leads to decreased pluralism and freedom of expression, many scholars, practitioners, and policy makers recognize that the phenomenon is more complicated than a simple, direct, causal relationship. Such complications are born from the fact that "nobody would deny that newspapers in a free and open society have to be privately owned. Only then can they be independent from outside influences" (von Dohnanyi & Mö ler, 2003, p. 22). As von Dohnanyi and Mö ler add,

---

[1] The case of *Rue89* in Chapter 5 will touch upon this acqi sition.

however, the market may challenge this independence, which is believed to be guaranteed by private ownership:

> Such independence, however, comes at a price. Publishers of privately owned news-papers have to generate enough business to withstand the normal pressure of com-petition, which is the lifeblood of any market economy. ().. The permanent conflict between the publisher's entrepreneurial right to react opportunistically to variable market conditions and the journalist's editorial freedom based on the concept of his basic human right to freedom of expression is the fundamental dilemma of the media business in general and of the newspaper industry in particular. (von Dohnanyi & Mö ler, 2003, p. 23)

As illustrated in the previous chapter, this permanent conflict is traditionally represented in media studies with an image of the so-called Chinese Wall between the newsroom and the management rooms or an image of the Church and the State. In times of decreasing circulation and significant changes in technologies for news production, distribution, and consumption, however, "the publisher's entrepreneurial right" has sometimes trumped journalistic pri-orities, inasmuch as many news organizations have found themselves in severe financial crisis and under threat of survival. With not enough money generated from the traditional business and organizational model of journalism, new solutions for reshuffling the compromise between management and journalism have been presented as urgent and even necessary. One solution for remedying the risk of disappearing newspapers is the construction of larger media groups, attained by acqi ring or merging smaller news organizations.

This chapter tells the story of *Göteborgs-Posten* (*GP—The Gothenburg Post*), a local newspaper in the second-largest city in Sweden. *GP* has existed for almost two centuries as a single newspaper company. At the beginning of 2000s, it found itself to be the flagship publication of the Stampen Group. Stampen is the largest media group in West Sweden and one of the largest in the country, with 37 local dailies at the highest count in 2012 (when many of the interviews for this study were conducted) although the number had decreased to 12 by 2020.

The journey that was this study started in the newsrooms of the local newspaper, where I investigated the development of new digital products. In developing a new product, launching it, and starting its production, I assumed, employees with different types of expertise would gather to discuss not only how they would realize the goal, but also what would make it a good product commercially, journalistically, and technically.

Following digital development at *GP*, I often came across references to Stampen, and traced them back in time and space: in time through secondary material and in space within the organization. While at *Il Sole-24 Ore*, I kept myself primarily within the boundaries and the walls of the newspaper. In

Gothenburg, I asked myself how the relationship between journalism and management was organized in such a large media group and what this meant, particularly for *GP*'s employeesa– nd not only those working in the news-room. This approach became even more interesting in 2015, when Stampen caught public attention for its financial difficulties and its need to reconstruct the company financially and when, in April 2019, the main owners, the Hjö ne family, lost its majority (Raviola, 2019).

In this chapter, I briefly present the story of *GP* and the main organizational compromise framing the relationship between journalism and management, as presented to me during my study. I then analyze how this relationship was enacted during three critical processes I followed in my research: (1) the development of new digital products at *GP* in 2011—2012; (2) the construction and growth of Stampen as a media group, especially after 2000; and (3) the financial reconstruction of Stampen between 2014 and 2016.

GÖTEBORGS-POSTEN

Göteborgs-Posten is the largest newspaper in Gothenburg, and its distribu-tion reaches the entire West Sweden Region. It has a daily print circulation of 177,000 copies and a weekly online reach of over 560,000 uniqe users. Following its vision of being "the world's best local newspaper", its coverage is dominated by locally relevant news, and the newspaper explicitly positions itself as giving voice to local communities.

GP was established in 1858 to serve the local area and is self-defined as having a strong brand and a strong relationship to the local community. After the bankruptcy of the competing newspaper, *Göteborgs Handels- och Sjöfartstidning*, in 1973, *GP* had a local monopoly on the news market. The changes in news consumption brought about by digital technologies have chal-lenged this monopoly, and *GP*'s print circulation decreased by 50% between 2008 and 2019 (Kantar Sifo, 2020; Nilsson & Weibull, 2010). Along with the print product, *Göteborgs Posten* has developed a number of digital products: a website (www.gp.se), a premium website (www.gp.se/gpplus), a mobile website, an iPhone app for news, an e-newspaper (*eGP*), and an iPad app focusing on photos (*GP Bild*). Most of the digital products have a relationship to the print newspaper, in the sense that they share content and brand, but *GP* has also entered other areas of the advertising and e-commerce market. In acqi ring *Dealie*, for example, a platform similar to *Let's Deal* or *Groupon*, it was able to offer high-discount coupons to consumers. At the beginning of this study, *GP* had about 350 employees, of which almost 200 were journalists sitting in the main newsroom.

After having belonged to several influential individuals in Gothenburg, *GP* was bought in 1926 by Harry Hjö ne, whose son, Lars, took over as the publisher and chief editor in 1969. In 1985, when Harry's grandchild, Peter Hjö ne, became *GP*'s CEO, he created Stampen AB, through which he bought out a number of smaller shareholders, thereby ensuring majority ownership of *GP* to the Hjö ne family. Between the mid-1990s and the end of the first decade of 2000s, under the energetic leadership of the new CEO, Tomas Brunegård, Stampen AB expanded significantly, and *GP* went from being "only a local actor in the hands of a liberal newspaper lord" to being, 20 years later "something totally different than a newspaper: a media house, an increasingly comprehensive group, with a foot in the digital world" (Greider, 2012). Fifty local newspapers in Sweden became part of the media group through direct acqi sitions or more complicated financial transactions. In less than 20 years, Stampen, whose majority owner was the Hjö ne family, with 74% shares held by Peter and 13% by his sister Marika Cobbold Hjö ne, had become one of the three largest media owners in Sweden, together with Bonnier and Schibsted. During this period, Peter was not only an active owner, but also worked as chief political editor (*politiske chefredaktör*) at *GP*. At the beginning of my field study in 2011, *GP* was one of the six business divisions in Stampen,[2] employing about 7,900 people (Lögr en, 2012).

By the end of 2012, Stampen had constructed a successful organization that had allowed *GP* and many other local newspapers to survive several recession periods and to realize cost savings. Just one year later, however, Stampen registered a loss of 862 million SEK and in 2016, majority owner Peter Hjö ne and the new CEO held a press conference announcing the media group's severe financial difficulties and its financial reconstruction.

In December 2016, after reconstruction, a new constellation of owners injected fresh capital into the media group. These Gothenburg-based investors financed an 81 million SEK capital increase, thereby acqi ring 50% of the capital; Peter Hjö ne kept 36.1% of the shares, and Marika Cobbold Hjö ne kept 7.6%. Rumors about a possible shift in Stampen's ownership intensified in the autumn of 2018, but it was not until April 2019 that a consortium of Nordic media companies was announced. It included Polaris Media,[3] NWT Group, and NK Media, which had become the majority owner in Stampen, with 51% of shares, limiting Peter Hjö ne's share to 14.6%.

---

[2]   The others were local newspapers in West Sweden (The West Coast Media Company), local newspapers in Central Sweden (Promedia), free newspapers (GISAB Company), new areas of development (Stampen Media Partner), and the printing and distribution division.

[3]   The Norwegian media group, Schibstedt, which owns the second biggest morning newspaper (*Svenska Dagbladet*) and the biggest evening newspaper (*Aftonbladet*) in Sweden, is the majority owner of Polaris Media.

NEWS FOR PROFIT: THE NEED TO MONETIZE
A DEMOCRATIC MISSION

Employees from different departments at *GP* had a relatively consistent view of what the company was and what it was doing: I was indeed surprised by the coherence of their narrative around what they were working for. When they talked about the relationship between journalism and business, they often stressed the fact that *GP* is and has always been a commercial enterprise, and although it is important to highlight that it also has a democratic mission, the company has continued to make a profit over the last 100 years. Alex, a former journalist, working in the Digital Development Group (DDG) and writing business cases of new digital products to propose to top management, told me that:

> The important thing for *GP* is not to risk its credibility; we have a common responsibility to readers. This role and this credibility is something we must maintain. We would never want anyone to think that *GP* is corruptt— hat we write something because we have these companies as big advertisers. But some of our readers think of us as a sort of half-public administration agency that will deliver news for free to everybody, and this is not the case. We are a commercial company and have been so since the 19th century. (Interview with Alex, April 2011)

In this qot e, Alex clearly stresses the fact that *GP* must make a profit and disassociates the newspaper from the idea held by certain readers that *GP* is a public agency, serving citizens. Although this is clear to many of the people I met at the newspaper, probably because of a deliberate strategy at the company and group level. I could, in fact, trace a past through my interviews in which the goal of serving everybody was explicitly expressed in the company's values. As Gaby, a marketing manager, told me a few years earlier, their core values used to be "local, credible, and for everybody", but then they made a change:

> … by choosing certain channels [e.g., iPhone and iPad], we exclude certain groups. So we have now chosen "open" [instead of "for everybody"] and it feels qi te good. It is not good to be for everybody. It can be difficult to develop products that have to be for "everybody". (Interview with Gaby, August 2011)

In this qot e, Gaby justifies moving away from "everybody" as a good shift in product development and *GP*'s presence in the market: From a marketing perspective, to be open is a better promise than the promise being for everybody, because it offers the possibility of differentiating products by market segment and pricing them differently.

Credibility is also mentioned as a key value at *GP*, as many of my interlocutors explained to me. As employees in all departments and at all levels of the organization stressed, *GP*'s credibility cannot be at risk, and it cannot be seen as a company that would tolerate any type of corruption. The importance of maintaining the asset that is *GP*'s brand value was seen as a way of developing the business. Credibility is closely related to brand, and the brand cannot be destroyed. Credibility is what allows *GP* to have readers in different media channels and seems to be what allows agreement between journalistic and business principles. Journalistic efforts, priorities, and peculiarities are justified as important for maintaining credibility. A credible brand encourages the reader to pay for the newspaper, thereby allowing *GP* to make profit. As Kim, a news editor said:

> Our agenda is to produce the content that people want and pay for, but it is also to unveil corruption in Gothenburg, because we have a democratic missionus working here. And it is clear that it is not possible to achieve it if nobody wants to pay for what we do, but many of those working at *GP* have several driving forces. We don't sell nails. *GP* is not a company that sells nails. Rather we want to achieve something without content. (Interview with Kim, April 2012)

If credibility is the highest organizational good that allows agreement between journalism and business at *GP*, the readership is often mentioned as proof of credibility. Readers could also be considered merely a route to profit. As Kim explained later, the role of a news editor is to contribute to the commercial side of *GP*—to maximize the number of readers, which the marketing department then monetizes.

Credibility, or in marketing terms, "the brand", is what allows *GP* to develop its business model. Readers pay in advance by subscribing to a product they cannot try or know about in advance, and, as a business developer at *GP* (a person responsible for exploring new markets) told me, this is "actually a fantastic business model, if you think about it".

Credibility as a higher principle is not the only factor that is functional to profit; according to business reasoning, more concrete choices defining the editorial line of the newspaper may be justified for their profitability. *GP*'s mission, as many interviewees often told me, was to be the best local newspaper in the world. The fact that *GP* is a local newspaper is one of its core values as well, which implies that the journalistic work should focus on the Gothenburg area. The increasing local focus is justified by the fact that digitization increases competition on national and international news coverage and by the fact that the organizational arrangement of the newsroom, which could do without a domestic national news section.

The relationships among departments, especially the newsroom, marketing, and IT are recognized as being much closer at the time of the study than they used to be. As Jin, a business manager, said:

> We have become much closer to each other in the various departments. Now we sit close to each other in some cases. For example Charlie [who works in marketing] is my neighbor; and also Robin, who is a technician; and Jessie, who is responsible for advertising. It is really a mixture of people with different backgrounds, but who understand each other. … In general, there is much more understanding for the different occupational roles. It is indeed journalism that makes it possible to sell advertisements and when the newspaper [circulation] is disappointing, then we need to go over to other products that have a future. (Interview with Jin, September 2011)

The general agreement at *GP* seemed to be that the newspaper is a commercial enterprise, dependent upon the market value of its journalistic credibility. This understanding, spread widely among departments and across hierarchical levels, also manifested itself in the way the organization of the newspaper changed over time. It was important, as one business developer stressed, to acknowledge that *GP* is not a public administration agency serving the general public, but a profit-making business. As a move to this shared understanding, some employees noticed a positive change in cooperation across departments. As Gaby, the marketing manager, explained to me:

> If we go back 20 years, journalists did not even say "hi" to people from marketing when meeting them in the elevator. They weren't worth it. Only in the last six years since I've been working here has there been another kind of cooperation, especially at the top management level. But the older the journalists and the more they do investigative journalism, the less they want to know what we do. (Interview with Gaby, August 2011)

Along the same line, others have talked about a culture of silos: Every department is a world of its own, and marketing and management cannot interfere with newsroom activities. Because the newsroom is considered the site of *GP*'s credibility, businesspeople also agree that they should not try to influence the content of the journalists' work but argue that the qe st for credibility sometimes becomes a bit extreme on the journalistic side. As Kai from marketing told me, *GP*'s editorial staff wrote an article about flea markets in the Gothenburg area, but failed to mention its own marketing department, which arranges a large flea market every year.

As Kai told me:

> Sometimes we don't communicate with each other because we don't have any informal meetings in the departments or across the departments, but it's better now since we got the common coffee lounge. Yet, we work in our different silos, and I would say that is [our] distinct [corporate] structure. (Interview with Kai, August 2011)

Kai was not alone in complaining about the silos. During the growth of Stampen as a media group, collaboration across boundaries became a mantra, and it was often said that the construction of the media group was built on an organizational model that "demanded collaboration and partnership for long-term growth and profitability" (*Stampen*, 2009, p. 1). In the next three sections, I explore how this idea of collaboration for growth and profitability unfolded at *GP* and at the group level.

EXPLORING INDEPENDENCE IN PRACTICE: COLLABORATION ACROSS BOUNDARIES

Having presented the way employees framed the overall organizational compromise between journalism and management, I now analyze how these frames were used to prioritize, justify, and evaluate actions taken to develop the company. Three areas of work are in focus here, following the trajectory of my field study and of Stampen: (1) the development of digital products at *GP*; (2) the strategy of Stampen's aggressive expansion; and (3) the reconstruction of the media group, following Stampen's severe financial difficulties. These three areas of work to develop *GP* and Stampen into a media group are justified by the urgency of technological development and by the conseqe nt projection of a dramatically different future for newspapers. The shifting ways of painting this futurea– s bright hope or dark despairs– eem to all point at the necessity of considering and evaluating the production of news in economic terms: Whether in good and bad times, news needs to be making money.

Developing Digital Products—or the Hope of Automation

The history of digital development at *GP* follows trends in the industry that are similar to those experienced at *Il Sole-24 Ore*. The Swedish newspaper launched its first web operations in 1995. During the 1990s, most of the digital projects came from the bottom rungs of the corporate ladder and were not systematically integrated into the main print news operations. As many of the employees told me during the interviews, people interested in digital developments were given the freedom and resources to experiment. Beginning in 2000, these projects became part of *GP*'s formal digital development strategy, and the digital operations were separated from the rest of the organization.

This separation into a dedicated unit was motivated by the recognition that the online world, especially the business side of the online world, works differently than the print world. At the beginning of the millennium, there was already a feeling of urgency at *GP* to find new sources of revenue, coupled with the belief that that revenue would probably come from the online world. As Ellis, a marketing manager, told me during an interview, digital development is "very much about compensating for the disappointing print circulation, with higher traffic and revenues through the digital channels" (Interview with Ellis, September 2011). Digital development and business value were closely paired at *GP*, which is why increasing revenues from digital channels and other sources became high priorities.

The digital business unit was separated from the newspaper operations until 2004. Sasha, an editor who had worked for the website, explained how digital and paper news production activities had been related until then:

> In the beginning, we could have two parallel or different worlds and we did not need to merge anything, between digital and newspaper. I have really fought for what is self-explanatory today [].. , because back then I worked with adding more content on the news website and nagged everyone to put out whatever content they had onto the web. (Lecture presentation by Sasha, May 2012)

Then the recession hit in 2004, and management decided to integrate the digital business into the rest of the organization, with an attempt to increase cooperation through cross-sectional meetings. This way of organizing was not considered beneficial to digital development, however, so in 2009 management decided to create a dedicated Digital Development Group (DDG), with the explicit purpose of tending to new opportunities and digital development. The DDG represents an attempt to formalize the digital development process within the company and to explore new business areas. Assigned to DDG, the program was called "100 *nya*" (100 new), a program spanning from 2009 to 2014, the goal of which was to create 100 million SEK of new revenue for the company.

The intention was that the DDG would encompass staff from the various departments within the organization, including business, editorial, and IT, with the plan that they, in turn, should help the development, while the rest of the organization remained the same. This way of organizing also enabled *GP* to merge business, editorial, and technological interests within one unit in order to encourage more cooperation and commercial thinking. The establishment of DDG has represented management's conscious effort to break down the walls of the various departments, in line with the cooperation-across-borders mantra of Stampen as a media group. Alex, a member of the DDG, explained the reasoning behind the creation of the DDG:

> Our head in the DDG is part of the editorial executive managementa– journalist from the beginning []... This was *GP*'s very tactical choice, because historically the editorial department has been very skeptical toward the commercial [aspect of the company]. So then you merge the worlds [].. , [because] everyone within his group [the DDG] belongs to either the IT, consumer, or corporate market department. (Interview with Alex, September 2011)

DDG has its own budget for developing new products. Every new product is evaluated through a business case, in which its economic feasibility and profitability is judged. As Alex explained:

> The development projects need to make money qi ckly. Of course you shouldn't do projects if they don't make any money, but it is very difficult to create, invent, implement, and then make money within a year. (Interview with Alex, September 2011)

Development projects chosen on the basis of their profitability may raise discussion at times. Jackie, an experienced newspaper editor, expressed disapproval for the development of *GP Listen*, an iPhone app that mechanically reads news. As Jackie said:

> DDG has qi te a lot of money for development—*GP Listen*, which they've developed, for example. I didn't think that we should put money into that, but they thought anyhow that it was a good idea and so they did it. Now there are qi te many that use it. Maybe I was wrong then.

Economic profitability within one year is not the only criterion for all the projects. *GP Bild*, for example, did not reached breakeven within one year, but it did receive the approval and the support of every part of the organization. It was developed, although there have been some discussions about the large number of staff involved and the appropriateness of the cost.

The gathering of people from different worlds for the development of new products in DDG triggered my curiosity. I had the sense that DDG and their product development would be an interesting site for an investigation of the relationship between journalism and management. I now present the story of how one digital product, *GP Bild*, was developed, particularly discussing how negotiations around the nature of the new product unfolded and how its production should be organized. *GP Bild* is an iPad app focused on pictures, the development of which involved a journalist, a designer, a technician, two photojournalists, a photo editor, and a business manager.

GP Bild—the photo application for the iPad
The iPad came to Sweden in time for Christmas 2010, following an international trend. In June 2010, *GP* had successfully launched its iPhone app; in the autumn of 2010, *GP*'s employees started thinking about possible developments for the iPad. As several employees tell it, the initial idea of an iPad app started with the weekend supplement *Två Dagar* (*Two Days*) and the goal of

creating an app with *feature* material. As Ingel, a member of the DDG, told me about this initial idea:

> The first generation of the iPad app built on *feature* material. We have a newspaper supplement called *Två Dagar*, where there's a lot of material on travel, fashion, etc. Our idea was to gather this feature material once a week and complete it with moving pictures, so we could do it rather flashily. (Interview with Ingel, May 2011)

The initial idea of an iPad app was closer to a magazine to be downloaded once a week than it was to a daily news app. As a graphic designer, Ingel designed a prototype of an app in which they would adapt the content of *Två Dagar* to the iPad:

> In such a big company as *GP*, content is produced once, here [for the print newspaper], and then adapted to the web and the mobile, so that, as a reader, you can find the same basic content when you surf the web in the evening or when you're sitting on the bus on your way home. (Interview with Ingel, May 2011)

With the prototype in their hands and with the help of the marketing department, DDG personnel made some calculations about costs and possible revenues. They concluded that it would be too expensive and not profitable, as two or three people would need to work on it full time. They needed something that reqi red fewer people and would cost less. The idea of a picture app, called *GP Bild*, was raised as a possible solution.

As Ingel told me while browsing through the iPad in search of the application to show me, the spark of this picture-based news app was Helle, a photographer who had worked at *GP* for a long time. "It was Helle that took up the idea. Helle knows all the material that *GP* has and doesn't use in everyday news production" (Interview with Ingel, May 2011). This idea was well received by the newsroom editors and the DDG, with the consideration that the apps that work on the iPad are usually highly visual and built around pictures. My interlocutors mentioned that they had other successful visual iPad apps in mind—ike *Life*; *CNN*; and the US public service radio, *NPA*.

GP Bild was meant to be distinct from the news mobile app, the website, and the newspaper, inasmuch as its design took its point of departure in photographs rather than the usual text. The purpose of the new app was to tell stories through pictures, by reversing the traditional newspaper order of priority between images and text:

> The idea is that you have a picture. You publish pictures. [Showing me the iPad] This is the latest picture. This is the one before the last one. This is the third last one. There is always a "stack" lying below in this way, and so you go through the pictures. Sometimes it can be a single picture. Sometimes it can be a picture gallery. (Interview with Ingel, May 2011)

The pictures came first and may be accompanied by a short text, appearing below the pictures and able to disappear behind double click. The text that accompanies the pictures would need to be short and easy to write and would not include links to the website articles, in order to reduce the opportunity for users to leave the appa– step that was considered undesirable. Having then obtained the agreement of the photographers and the DDG business developer on the basic logic of the app, Ingel started to design the app concretely. The idea behind *GP Bild* was a simple one, which should correspond with the simplicity of the production work. As Ingel put it:

> … The intention is that most of what we do should not be a lot of work. Today they already do photo galleries for the web, and they'll be included in the flow. They'll be made in the same way as the other photo galleries. Also on the iPhone app. … I don't need to have an idea of costs. But it must be simple for the readers to find; it must be simple to publish. (Interview with Ingel, May 2011)

Although the designer is not responsible for the costs and profitability of the app, Ingel is convinced that the simplicity of the concept and its production and its user-friendliness are related. Several people noted the simplicity, which encompasses understandability and usefulness for the readers and reqi res little labor, making it cheap to produce. Alex from the DDG emphasized that, after rejecting the option of a feature magazine app as too expensive to produce, this kind of app was chosen in light of the limited resources needed, particularly in terms of journalistic work. Pictures exist in-house and *GP Bild* would simply offer the opportunity to reuse them:

> The idea is that it shall be really simple to publish. One publishes a certain number of pictures from the existing editorial system, and this is done mathematically, automatically. It shouldn't be edited. (Interview with Alex, August 2011)

GP Bild is built in html5. This markup language for presenting content on the World Wide Web allows content to be accessible in a similar (recognizable and readable) way on different media. As Ingel put it, they want to try to "build it on html5 to then be able to take the same content and show it on the web in the same way". The first and second version offered the possibility of showing pictures in galleries under six categories: Gothenburg, Sweden, World, Culture and Entertainment, Sports, and Readers' Pictures.

Both the DDG and the leading newsroom team at *GP* had prioritized simplicity in their goal of publishing content in a different format. The increasing number of publication formats and devicespa per, e-paper, website, mobile app, and iPad app—reqi red increased editing efforts. At the beginning of the mobile app, for example, a desk journalist worked all day to adjust the titles of the article to the mobile format, so they would not look strange on a smaller screen. News editor Kim described this extra work:

> We're looking for structures. We know that there's an increase in the *efterarbete* [extra work] we need to do after we have identified a piece of news. The planning of the channels takes a lot of work, so we also need to plan our resources in accordance with that, and then it helps of course to know the length of time different things take. (Interview with Kim, April 2012)

Kim added that when they opened up a two-way communication channel with the readersw- ith a blog and comments, for examplet— he work increased significantly. Responding and moderating the readers' comments, planning how news should be distributed in different channels, and writing for different channels are all new practices of news production that need to be staffed and organized. As Kim explained, they needed to design a media dramaturgy, in which a given investigation could be appropriately sliced up. They had to consider what should be published on paper or website, what should be complimentary to customers, what should be part of the premium package, and how they could use pictures in *GP Bild*. The idea was to divide an investigation into parts and sort them into different channels.

This effort of dividing and sorting was part of the "afterwork". When the category of afterwork is discretely constructed, a smooth way opens up for automation: The afterwork is what can and should be automated without endangering journalistic qa lity. It is the editing for different formats that is the primary target of automation:

> And it is clear that as we have a big bouquet of different channels, it takes too much work and is not profitable to sit and [manually] chop everything. And this is not content work, we call it editing. So this has to happen with more automation. On the contrary, content is content and we don't automatize content work. So it is about making the presentation [of content] smarter and more efficient. (Interview with Kim, April 2012)

Automation thus holds the hope of saving time and money, while simultaneously freeing journalists from tedious work and allowing them to focus on their real vocation. A great deal of work is dedicated to building the technical structure and the routines, however, in order to save future work: Not to work reqi res a lot of work.

Automation in the hope of reducing costs and increasing the scale of production on multiple channels was in line with the strategy for building Stampen as a media group. Common technologies across newspapers, allowing the publication of content across platforms and titles, are often mentioned in the media group's annual reports as necessary factors to allow *GP* to capitalize on the advantages of the expansion. In the next section, I explore the growth of Stampen as a media group by analyzing the way in which the intensive acqi - sitions were justified.

From "One Man, One Newspaper"[4] to "One Team, Many Newspapers"

Since my first encounter with *GP* and the DDG in 2011, I was amazed by the enthusiasm and confidence that my interlocutors expressed in the future of newspapers and specifically of their own media group. It did not take long for them to clarify that all of *GP*'s digital development was to be understood within the world of Stampen, comprising many local newspapers, partners, and allies. The first meeting I had in the newspaper house in Polhemsplatsen in Gothenburg was with Chris, a member of Stampen's top management team, a former journalist, who was, at the time, responsible for business develop-ment. Given my experience at *Il Sole-24 Ore*, where I followed the daily prac-tical newswork, I remember having been surprised by the tone and theme of my conversation with Chris, who seemed to be occupied by issues that would probably go under the label of strategy and concerned the broad directions for the media group's business development. This was not surprising, given Chris's position, but a little confusing for me, looking for the details of every-day organizing. I later understood, by getting closer to the everyday organizing of digital development at *GP*, that digital development was conceived as part of something biggerS- tampen—and that it had to be understood as such. So, in this section I analyze how the construction of the media group was narrated and how the relationship between journalism and management was framed in these narratives.

My aim here is not to describe in detail all the steps that led to the con-struction and growth of Stampen, but rather to highlight how this construction implied a certain way of negotiating value and actions between journalism and management. To give the reader an idea of the size and speed of the expansion, it will suffice to qot e here an extract from *Avstampet: The Story of the Growth and Success of a Media Group* (Westgårdh & Johnsson, (2012), a book written by two Stampen journalists and published by Stampen. After telling about Stampen's acqi sitions and other directions of expansion, primarily from

---

4   "One man, one newspaper" was a saying commonly attributed to Harry Hjö ne, who bought *GP* in 1926. Harry was the grandfather of Peter Hjö ne, who had succeeded in the newspaper ownership and leadership, following his grandfather Harry and his father Lars. Among other sources, this saying is reported by Westgårdh and Johnsson (2012) in their book *Avstampet: The Story of the Growth and Success of a Media Group* and in the Gothenburg City Theatre piece "The newspaper house that God forgot", per-formed in 2017.

the point of view of the CEO, top management, and the majority owner, the authors summarized their achievement:

> No matter where their desk is nowadays, both Tomas [Brunegård] and Peter [Hjö ne] can look out at a media landscape where their common efforts have resulted in a clear change and in a position that hardly anyone thought was possible when the "New Burger"[5] entered the newspaper house for the first time 20 years ago (pp. 3043 05).
> Then there was Gö eborgs-Posten and not much more. Today Gö eborgs-Posten is one of the group's six business divisions. Apart from the second largest morning newspaper [in Sweden], the group includes a hundred companies with an overall turnover of about 5 billion [SEK, ~500 million EUR] and about 7,000 employees. At the beginning of the summer of 2012, the group looked like this in its entirety:
>
> • Promedia, which consists of 14 subscription-based local newspapers and two free newspapers in [two counties in Central Sweden] ()..
> • The media company, West Coast, with five local media houses ().. and the free newspapers *VarbergsPosten, Vänersborgaren, FalkenbergsPosten, Trollhättan 7 dagar,* and *Halmstad 7 dagar.*
> • GISAB, Free Newspapers in Sweden Inc., with 31 local free newspapers in the larger metropolitan area of Stockholm, with a weekly circulation of 900,000. ()..
> • V-TAB, the largest Nordic printing company, with operations in 11 sites in Sweden and prints daily newspapers, magazines, direct advertising, and produces sign and retail advertising, books, and catalogs. Big newspaper clients are *Göteborgs-Posten, Aftonbladet, Expresse, Svenska Dagbladet, Dagens Industri,* and *Metro.*
> • Stampen Media Partner, that leads the development of the group within the segments Life Style Media, Social Media, Editorial Media, Mobile Media, Experience Media, and Outdoor Media. In Life Style Media there is the blog network, Devote; the websites Familjeliv and Brö lopstorget;[6] and the sport site, Svenska Fans. Within the Mobile Media there are the digital agencies Adeprimo and Mobiento, which work with mobile marketing and Adientot— he Nordic leading actor within mobile advertising. Within Editorial Media, is the business media publisher, Appelberg Publishing Group. Finally, there is the segment, Outdoor Media ().. , specializing in advertising in public transportation, in parking lots and in magazine distributions at Swedish airports.

Besides the six business divisions mentioned here, there were a number of other centralized functions to support the overall administration of the group and its development. In Stampen's 2011 Annual Report, the media group,

---

[5]   *Nyburgare* (New Burger) was the nickname given to Brunegård when he was recruited as *GP*'s CEO in 1996. He had previously been Vice CEO for Burger King Sweden.
[6]   Two of the earliest and largest user-generated-content websites in Sweden. Their focus is family life and weddings.

"which is today Sweden's biggest owner of local daily newspapers" (Stampen, 2011, p. 38), was represented.

The construction of Stampen as a media group was driven by Peter Hjö ne's logic: "Those who don't eat are eaten" (Westgårdh & Johnsson, 2012). He wanted to find a way to "strengthen our own capacity so that we would not be swept away by the wind or the big players" (Westgårdh & Johnsson, 2012, p. 16). The CEO and the main owner of Stampen were both convinced that *GP* would not have survived the crisis of the first decade of the 2000s if it had not been "embedded in a successful media group" (Westgårdh & Johnsson, 2012, p. 326). CEO Tomas Brunegård stressed the profit advantage of belonging to the group:

> I think that *GP* would have gone bankrupt in the last business cycle, if we had not had the Stampen Group. If we had just had *GP*, I think we would not have survived the crisis. It would never have worked. What horrible losses we would have made... One needs to go back to the early '70s to find numbers that low. ().. Today *GP* is much in a much better state than [it has been] in the last 15 years. There have not been many times that the newspaper has earned as much money as in September and October 2010. We earned over 20 million [SEK] per month; therefore we have basically done something [good]. (Westgårdh & Johnsson, 2012, p. 326)

Brunegård was unanimously recognized as the motor behind the construction of Stampen, and there is no shortage of texts in media and annual reports where he explained his ideas during this process. The overall impression from all these texts from the time of Stampen's expansion is that Stampen was to be considered an economic construction to be highly valued for its profit-making ability, and the responsibility for this construction was on the side of managers and directors rather than editors.

The growth of Stampen reqi red a complicated web of relationships among a large number of companies: Some local newspapers were acqi red 100% by Stampen, becoming its subsidiaries; others were co-acqi red by Stampen and other Swedish media groups, creating new companies. A "Stampen sphere", as many called it, was therefore created, with companies directly and indirectly, fully and partially owned by Stampen. When I approached *GP*, my interlocutors made clear to me that the local newspaper is not a small ship in the large and stormy ocean of media industries, but that its development is part of a large, powerful, and growing ship called Stampen. The "Stampen sphere" was an intricate network of allies that were the preferred collaborators in developing new products and that represented the possibility of making *GP* products bigger than *GP* itself, by sharing them with other newspapers. One of the DDG members explained this logic of collaboration within Stampen at *GP*:

> If we go back to '94– 95, then everybody [all the newspapers] did everything by themselves. We produced everything ourselves, except for a little bit of TT news [the Swedish national news agency], but in principle, everything was produced in this house. We printed ourselves, we owned the printing presses, and we distributed ourselves. The printing business has become just few big businesses. We own one via Stampen; Bonnier has another one. It is not part of our core operations any longer; the distribution companies are owned together.

Printing and distribution were centralized early and qi ckly under the direction of Tomas Brunegård and through partnerships and joint ventures with other local actors in the media landscape. Significant savings in these areas appeared in annual reports, thus confirming the goodness of that consolidation strategy. Despite the early centralization of printing and distribution, it was not until the acqi sition of the so-called "Center Party Newspapers" that Stampen significantly restructured its organization and became a media group working for common development in all directions, according to the accounts of people working with it. The acqi sition came at a high price, howeverove r 1,800 million SEK (~180 million EUR)a– s Westgårdh and Johnsson (2012, p. 231) reported in their book that Peter Hjö ne's father, Lars, said of this acqi sition: "I would wake up during the night and fence with my arms and scream because it was such an awful lot of money."

Like printing and distribution, new business development was an area that could be centralized, and in 2006 the business development company, Mycket Media, was founded as part of the Stampen constellation. This company was owned 78% by Stampen and 22% by other Swedish media groups, and its goal was to facilitate common development for all its owners. But for Stampen, this acqi sition translated into the possibility of developing digital products, testing them in one newspaper, and then making them available for the others.

As Lee, one of the editors working with digital development at *GP* explained to me, Mkt Media and Stampen functioned like the European Union. Mkt Media was like the European Commission, setting priorities and making suggestions on common areas of development for its shareholders' newspapers. The various media companies were, in turn, like the European member states, which financially supported the common Mkt Media organization, representatives of which took part in a number of advisory committees held by Mkt Media, to propose and discuss development projects. Once a project was prioritized, it was placed and managed by one of the local newspapers and co-financed by the newspaper and Mkt Media. The development of a mobile news app for the iPhone, for example, was realized by the DDG at *GP* and co-financed by *GP* and Mkt Media. Once the app was created, it was made available in the Mkt Media's product portfolio: The other local newspapers belonging to Mkt Media's shareholders could buy the app and adapt it to their content for a discounted price, and other external newspapers could purchase it. Jin, a member of the DDG at *GP*, explained the advantages of this way of organizing development work:

> ... the idea is that you develop [a product] once and then everybody can re-use it. And it means that in the best of worlds, let's say that something costs 100 to develop, we [*GP*] don't need to put more than 30 into it, and the rest can be taken centrally. So when the next [newspapers from Stampen] buy it, it costs maybe 5, because the costs for conceptualizing are already paid and the cost is then very low to adapt the digital solution [to the local newspaper].

My analysis of field material and secondary accounts of the growth of Stampen is consistently pointing at an important conseqe nce for the relationship between journalism and management in the Swedish media group. Stampen was a construction that needed to be maintained and sustained, which reqi red a great deal of work, new to the formerly independently owned local newspapers. As Mika, working at Mkt Media, told me during an interview:

> Since the construction of Mkt Media, Stampen has increased its investment in commercial activities. There are more and more people working with business relations. ... They take care of the overall business aspects. Earlier there was a development advisory board that had its own business group [at *GP*]. This became a little bit unnecessary, because Stampen has employed people that work with these things on a daily basis. So today, the business issues are driven from Stampen. (Interview with Mika, April 2011)

As Mika noted, the business work has not only intensified, but also has become Stampen's own area of jurisdiction, rendering much of the local newspapers' individual and independent business development work redundant. Although the core of the group was framed as "local newspapers", and focused on the West Sweden region, what seemed to occupy most of the time and energy in the construction of the group was the realization of synergies and economies of scale through the centralization of certain functions, as represented. This also meant a change in terms of the most important role in newspaper organizations. During his trips to the US, Tomas had observed the development within the American media industry, where consolidation of the industry was considered to be in a new and more intensive phase with more and more newspapers that are included in stronger conglomeratesgr oups rather than family businessesa nd where managers and directors were at least as important as editors. As Tomas Brunegård recounted in Westgårdh and Johnsson (2012), "I said this to Lennart Hö ling, that this will happen here as well, but he just laughed at me". (p. 139)

Stampen's Crisis: When "Something Bigger" Falls

All the enthusiasm and confidence that I observed in my interlocutors during 2011 and 2012 seems to have disappeared just a couple years later. As described in the report, "Winners and losers of the newspaper game", broadcast on Swedish public service television in April 2015.[7]

> It's the media industry fair [here in Gothenburg], the meeting point of a sector moving against the wind. It's a difficult time for everybody. Google and Facebook take advertising money; the mobile and social media take readers. And Peter Hjö ne's Stampen has done the worst, with the biggest loss in Swedish newspaper history, more than one billion [SEK, ~100 million EUR] over the last two years. (Uppdragsgranskning, 2015)

The newspaper crisis, which has been feeding a global debate for at least 20 years, has had many local variations of hopes, struggles, and despair. Consolidation of ownership through a consistent number of acqi sitions has been a story of hope for Stampen, until the foundations of the construction of "something bigger" got shaken by financial troubles that seemed to appear suddenly. This section analyzes how the story of Stampen turned from hope to despair over a short period and how the relationship between journalism and management got framed during this time.

The analysis in this section is based primarily on the public debate around Stampen's difficulties between 2010 and 2017, particularly showing how the justifications for building Stampen as "something bigger" turned into the reasons for its failure. These justifications confirm and make visible the overall organizational compromise between journalism and managementi— n this case as "news for profit".

During Stampen's aggressive expansion, few people had raised their voices in concern for the group's solidity, as many of the acqi sitions had been financed by bank loans. But traces of a critiqe were visible in some of the annual reports, in which Brunegård responded with confidence on the sustainability of its own construction: "It turned out that the Cassandras that saw a bad omen in a scrappy over-leveraged media group without any chance of realizing synergy advantages, were terribly wrong" (Stampen, 2010, p. 4). In the 2011 annual report, Brunegård deemed it appropriate to deny the excessive

---

[7]   Parts of this study of Stampen's crisis were also presented in Raviola (2019).

proportion of goodwill value in Stampen's income statement. But an interview with Brunegård appears to have been staged in the report:

> Question: Goodwill makes up for more than half of Stampen's assets. Is it a problem that there is seemingly so much air in the income statement?
> Answer: In this industry, you buy brands and attract brains. Such things are not visible in the income statement and therefore goodwill emerges. The fact is that Stampen's income statement has never been stronger than now, and we have exceeded our solidity goal of 30%. (Stampen, 2011, p. 5)

Despite these and other traces of critiqe , it was not until the end of 2013 that Stampen, often presented as a success at international newspaper conferences and praised for having found a way to provide survival to many local news-papers in gloomy times, saw its shining growth suddenly arrested. The 2013 income statement reported a total loss of 862 million SEK (~86.2 million EUR), ascribed mainly to the fact that goodwill assets of earlier acqi sitions, which had been partially written off over the years, were finally consistently written off (af Kleen, 2014, May). In the summer of 2014, banks reqi red Stampen to repay 600 million SEK (~60 million EUR) of its loans, which caused a liqi dity crisis within the corporation. Several actions were taken to remedy this crisis in the following years: The organization was restructured, separating paper and online operations; downsizing plans were implemented; acqi red companies were sold below cost; and a new CEO was appointed. These steps resulted in a significant loss in Stampen's income statement and decreased the solidity of the company, which was reported as falling from 22% in 2013 to about 7.8% in 2015 (Lundin, 2015). Then banks demanded that Stampen repay its 600 million SEK debt.

Banks encouraged the goodwill devaluation, because they did not see that the value of acqi red companies were realizing corresponding economic gains over the years. As Brunegård said:

> We will adjust ourselves this year and will decrease the goodwill values in Stampen's balance sheet. We still believe in newspapers and their ability to create value and make profit. (Tomas Brunegård, Interview with *Medievärlden*, 16 December 2013)

In the public debate, Stampen's top managementpa rticularly the owner, Peter Hjö ne, and the expansion-period CEO, Tomas Brunegård, are con-sidered primarily responsible for "having overbought" by making the wrong calculations and acqi ring too much with borrowed money. One of the biggest and most scrutinized was the acqi sition of the Center Party Newspaper Group, in 2005 for 1.8 billion SEK (~180 million EUR). After this acqi sition, Stampen's debt increased sevenfold, reaching 1 billion SEK (~100 million EUR), (*Uppdragsgranskning*, 2015), and the solidity of the group fell to from

35.6% in 2004 to 22.2% in 2005. Then-CEO Tomas Brunegård explained the rationale behind the acqi sition strategy by appealing to the necessity of building a competitive advantage for the future:

> We in Sweden have a very strong tradition of local newspapers. It has remained strong, but competition has become stronger and will be even stronger in the future. It will come from free newspapers, national media, Google – newcomers in short – and we want to lead the development in all this through a stronger collaboration and the creation of the conditions for a better competitive advantage. (From *Mittnytt*, 2005, in *Uppdragsgranskning*, 2015)

As described in the previous section, Brunegård saw the acqi sition as a way to increase Stampen's presence in the market, rendering it stronger on the business side. He saw the acquisitions as necessary in order to survive. As I observed elsewhere (Raviola, 2019), this market frame was based on future expectations of how the media would evolve and what organizational form would be suitable to journalism in the future. There was pressure to expand, with the belief that this would realize advantages on the business side: Acqi sitions were considered "a calculated risk", in order to guarantee a future to the newspaper rather than extravagant impulse shopping. As one of the directors on the board said, "There was a very strong belief in the future and the feeling that one should build something, that one had built something big and that one would build something that was even bigger" (*Uppdragsgranskning*, 2015). As Peter Hjö ne explained to a reporter who challenged him on the appropriateness of all those acqi sitions:

> Reporter: Did you reflect upon each acqi sition?
> Peter Hjö ne: Yes, if you think we ran around with some sort of mass media shopping chart and just threw things we found on our way into it, that is a totally absurd thought. We have taken, and feel that we've taken, a big responsibility for mass media development, for our position in it. And we have done this with consideration, and we have done it with calculation, and we have done it with the approval of the banks along the way, and we were certainly not alone in this kind of judgment. Yes, sure, we have thought carefully and calculatedly. But everything does not become exactly the way one had thought. It is just afterward that it becomes how one had thought. (*Uppdragsgranskning*, 2015)

About a year later, at the announcement of the reconstruction, Peter Hjö ne recognized that Stampen's problems were not related to the running of the news operations, but rather the "backpack of debt that we carry, primarily after the acqi sition of the Center Newspapers" (Syrén, Carlsson, & Thunborg, 2016). The desire to make greater profits, save more money, and generate larger revenues by means of expansive acqi sitions had damaged the single newspapers and decreased their ability to generate profit independently.

In December 2015, the situation got worse (Raviola, 2019). In fact, following a European Union ruling settled in 2010 about a 6% tax rate for printing services, the Swedish Higher Court decided to apply the same tax rate in Sweden, lowering it from the previous 25%. Stampen owns one of Sweden's largest printing plants and had counted over the years on a 25% tax rate for its customer: Now the group was suddenly in debt with the Swedish Tax Agency (STA) for a value of 375 million SEK (~37.5 million EUR), which would be returned to the customers. STA wanted the money, but so did the banks. This resulted in a significant loss in Stampen's income statement and decreased the solidity of the company, which was reported to be falling from 22% in 2013 to about 7.8% in 2015 (Lundin, 2015). Banks, in turn, demanded that Stampen pay off 600 million SEK (~60 million EUR) of debt. Martin Alsander, Stampen's CEO since 2014, described the beginning of 2016 to Marie Kennedy:

> In early 2016 we were forced to deal with the liqi dity issue, and we started making acqa intance with the notion of reconstruction. We could not both pay off our loans to the banks and pay taxes. We did need a plan for doing both. (Kennedy, 2016, pp. 2021)

In May 2016, Stampen started a financial reconstruction process: "the largest [Swedish] reconstruction after Saab Automobile, taking into account the number of employees" (Olander & Hofbaue, 2016, p. 8). The decision was announced to employees on the same day, who were called via the Intranet to a morning personnel meeting with information on the future of Stampen from the board of directors and top management. The public received the news via a press conference.

A financial reconstruction is an alternative path to filing for bankruptcy; it is aimed at saving companies that have severe financial difficulties, but are believed to have some hope for survival (Raviola, 2019). The reconstruction process, led by a court-assigned reconstructor, usually implies the creditors' consent to cede part of their claims. During this process, Stampen has managed to sell many of the group's newspapers over the past few years, reduce its financial debt from about 1 billion SEK (~100 million EUR) to 380 million SEK (~38 million SEK) and negotiate a new agreement with both the banks and STA (Raviola, 2019).

In order to succeed in the financial reconstruction, the group had to show its creditorspr imarily the banks and the statet— hat it was able to make significant savings. Hjö ne and Brunegård had justified the expansion as a necessity for survival; it would allow for cost savings for printing, development, and distribution. As it noted, however, the coordination advantages were overestimated (Lapidus, 2014), and in the face of the financial crisis, the costs of news operations were considered too high. Consequently, more than 400 employees were laid off, publication freqe ncy decreased, printing plants closed or were sold, and functions centralizeda– ll in the name of saving costs and surviving the crisis. As Stampen's new CEO, Martin Alsander, explained:

> We are present in 40 towns, and it is clear that perhaps it is not optimal to have a 7-day newspaper in all of them ().. In printing operations, you want to have fewer production units and optimize publications to fewer days. And in this way reduce the costs. (af Kleen, 2014, May)

Stampen's employees and other journalists expressed worried reactions over this solution. A lower publication freqe ncy, in fact, is claimed to lead to a further reduction of newsroom personnel, making even more journalists redundant.

Another recurrent discussion in the debate around Stampen's crisis revolved around the excessive salaries, bonuses, and dividends to top managers and directors, with Tomas Brunegård and Peter Hjö ne acqi ring the highest compensation. As I noted elsewhere (Raviola, 2019), the number-full public debate was oriented to demonstrate how a small group of people at Stampen became rich while taking the company into collapse. This debate reveals how the work of managers and directors was valued vis-à-vis that of other categories of employees and of other companies. Brunegård, who came from Burger King and had not grown up in the newspaper business, had indeed predicted that managers and directors would become just as important as editors in newspaper companies. For Brunegård, turning newspapers into economic entities was an inevitable sign of change; whereas for others in the industry, the excessive salaries and bonuses of managers and directors was a sign of decadence. In his reportage on the fall of the old Swedish newspaper barons, renowned journalist Bjö n af Kleen wrote:

> 2004 – the year of the acqi sition of the Centre Newspapers – Stampen paid about 16 million [SEK: ~1.6 million EUR] in dividends to the owners and 2.7 million [SEK: ~.27 million EUR] to the directors and top managers in salary and compensation.
>
> 2012 – the dividends had increased to 48 million [~SEK: 4.8 million EUR] to the owners and about 21 million [SEK: 2.1 million EUR] in salary to directors and top managers. (af Kleen, 2014, December, p. 56)

While the journalist used the time comparison to show the excessive level of compensation, Stampen's owner considered time the precise reason why directors' and top managers' salary could not be treated as too high. When qe stioned about the multimillionaire salaries received by Brunegård, then CEO, he responded:

> One can always discuss the level of compensation, but I don't really want to comment on single individuals. I can only note that the agreement was signed in another time, with other future predictions than those that became reality. (Syrén et al., 2016, p. 16)

Bjö n af Kleen then pushed Peter Hjö ne about the time comparison, and he responded:

> I am not stupid, nor deaf, nor blind. And I can understand that you have opinions about high salaries if you don't have it yourself.
> But it is time to make the debate more reasonable. During my grandfather's time, one paid almost no dividends. But I don't think it is a reasonable approach today, if one wants to have some shareholders remaining. When I look back at the last 10 years, I can observe that we have paid out, on average, 9.2% of our internally generated resources. If one had done an evaluation of the group, sold it, and placed the money somewhere else, the return would have been very much higher. (af Kleen, 2014, December, p. 58)

As Hjö ne's reasoning shows, both the past and other companies were used as terms of comparison to frame the excessive level of compensation – salaries, dividends, and bonuses. The q estion then was on which type of company constitutes the correct comparison. Stampen's owner claimed that the comparison should be with any other company, in terms of return on investment and top managers' salaries. "Shareholders in a media company do not need to settle for less than what the general market gives": This is what Hjö ne argued in *Uppdraggranskning* (2015). Otherwise, it would be difficult to recruit valid managers and shareholders (Raviola, 2019).

Establishing the need for a different relationship between journalism and management, others compared Stampen to other news organizations, considering them special types of organizations for their role in democracy rather than regular economic entities. Along this line, the compensation received by Stampen's top management, directors, and owners were significantly higher than for other similar organizations, which constituted a sign of the dominance of business over journalism. Tomas Brunegård's monthly compensation as a directora– part-time positionw– as 492,000 SEK (~49,200 EUR) per month: "SVT's [the Swedish public service broadcaster] president receives, as a term of comparison, a qa rter of that amount. Per year" (af Kleen, 2014,

May). Many journalists covering Stampen's crisis expressed explicit moral disapproval of top managers' and directors' excesses:

> At the same time there is news about the crisis of the newspaper industry. *Journalisten* [journalists' union magazine] has published the list of the chief editors and owners who have earned the most over the past years. The fact the *DN*'s [the largest national morning newspaper] Gunilla Herlitz received 19 million SEK [~1.9 million EUR] led to an uproar in the newsroom last year, but she ends up in only 6th place. The list is led by Stampen's majority owner Peter Hjö ne and by Hallpressens' President Lovisa Hamrin, both with a total income of more than 70 million SEK [~7 million EUR] during the period 20092013. This shows that the most serious crisis of the daily press is not economic. It is intellectual and moral. (Lindgren, 2015, p. 61)

This disapproval is directed not only to Stampen, but also to other media companies which have taken the path of managerialization. As one commentator explained: "Like so many other media companies, Stampen has lost its organizational culture and become just as 'corporate' as any other publicly listed company" (Aagård, 2014, p. 5). The reconstruction made the blaming of Stampen's top managers and directors' excesses even more severe, as they were juxtaposed to the number of people losing their jobs and not being paid during the same period.

DISCUSSION: MAKING NEWS FOR PROFIT IN GOOD AND BAD TIMES

The story of the rise and fall of Stampen shows a different model for organizing independence than does the separation described in Chapter 3. For Stampen, the crisis of the news industry was a justification for embarking on an aggressive expansion and fight against decreasing newspaper circulation by eating up all the surrounding smaller newspapers and other companies. These acqi sitions aimed at increasing profitability of the media group was simultaneously confirming the economic value of news operations and the financial validity of the construction of Stampen by means of the market values of the acqi sitions. Stampen introduced an overarching and growing structure of organizational functions that were dedicated to supporting the administration of the media group and moving its business development forward. Not only did this structure create no new types of work in line with making news for profit; it also increased the distance between newsrooms and top management and the interdependence of newspaper subsidiaries.

The analysis of field material and public debate presented in this chapter illustrates a case in which management not only becomes another way of valuing and prioritizing actions in the expansion of a media group, but its principles of worthpr imarily efficiency and profitbe come common higher goods for the whole organization. This is indeed a contested process, and the compromise of making news for profit as a survival necessity needs to be re-established and confirmed repeatedly. Once established in the organization, however, and assigned to a dedicated group of guardianst— op management, directors, and the employees of the overarching Stampen structuret— his compromise seemed ironically to confirm itself in both good and bad times. In good times, increasing profit was the proof that this compromise is the valid way to go and should even be reinforced with further expansion. In bad times, profitability becomes the principle against which news production needs to be judged, and changes in the organization, like downsizing and rationalizing, were justified.

4. Entrepreneurial journalism and the dream of a new independence: making money for the news

I remember the first time we[1] met the founders of *Rue89*: Gabriel, Jules, and Dominiqe .[2] They told us they were journalists and entrepreneurs. This combination was new to me; until then I had primarily studied established newspapers and learned about the importance of avoiding contamination between the Company and the Newsroom, as I discussed in Chapter 2. I was puzzled. What did this mean in practice? How did they reconcile their reputations as journalists with their activities as entrepreneurs, business owners, and managers? This chapter tells the story of an entrepreneurial journalistic venture and a dream of a new independence.

Entrepreneurship has entered the domain of journalism following a general trend. As the mission statement states on the website of *Politico*, a US-based political journalism company founded in 2007:

> … we live in an entrepreneurial age, not an institutional one. Until recently, most reporters derived their impacta– nd often their sense of professional esteemf– rom the prestige and gravity of the organizations they worked for. The Web, among other forces, has demolished much of the comparative advantage that big newspapers and networks once enjoyed. Today, many of the reporters having the most impact are those whose work carries a uniqe signature, who add a distinct voice to the public conversation. Their work, in other words, matters more than where they work. (Harris & VandeHei, 2007)

Politico's editor-in-chief, John Harris, and the executive editor, Jim VandeHei, wrote that statement. They had previously worked at the *Washington Post* but

---

[1]   The study of *Rue89* was conducted in collaboration with Professor Pablo Boczkowski, whose expertise, contacts and legitimacy were key to get access and discuss some of the field material. I express my sincere gratitude to him for this opportunity.

[2]   Like all other names given to my interlocutors in this book, these names are invented by me. In all other cases, I have also kept all my interlocutors gender-neutral in order to ensure the protection of their identity. In this case, however, as all the founders of *Rue89* were male and they were publicly known, I do not hide their gender in this chapter and the next one.

had left to start a new political website, financed by the owner of the media company Capitol Hill. Their mission statement seems to say that journalists can and do work outside big newspapers and television networks because they can publish their work independent of the established media on the web. They can be entrepreneurs outside the institutionalized media.

The link between entrepreneurship and independence has been a significant one for many other so-called "pure players" around the world. That label became popular in the first decade of 2000s and referred to news organizations like *Huffington Post* that operate purely or at least primarily online. In 2009, pure players in France formed the lobbying and trade association, the French Association for Independent Online News Producers (Spiil). As I became more familiar with the talk and actions of entrepreneurial journalists in France, I realized that members of Spiil held a common belief that entrepreneurship was the new route to independence. This becomes clear when looking at the program of the seventh annual Day of the Independent Online Press, organized in Paris in December 2016 by Spiil. The press release summarizing the day was entitled: "Making enterprise in the press sector: The reasons for believing in it", and it described the discussions as:

> This 7th day of the online press has also been the occasion for Spiil to reinforce its engagement around the notion of *independence*. The association has highlighted the fact that the profitability of the press's enterprises was one of the primary guarantees of this independence. This observation is shared with other associations gathering news and cultural enterprises (radios and televisions with the SIRTI, book publishers with the International Alliance of independent publishers).
> This day has also fulfilled its objective: to show that press entrepreneurs continue to believe in the value of information and rely on this value to build profitable economic models. (Spiil, 2016)

As stated in the Spiil's press release, profitability is understood as a means of achieving and upholding independence—the highest principle of journalism. Many entrepreneurial journalists want to combine economic and editorial independence and prove that making independent qa lity news online can be sustainable. This was also the case with *Rue89*, which, like many other pure players, started in France during the same wave. In 2011, a cinema critic and journalist directed a film entitled *La Rue est à eux*. In an interview with me in May 2011, she said:

> For a film director, *Rue89* is a more interesting object [than other pure players]— more complexw- hich raises more qe stions. And the boss is also nicer. ().. In any case I wanted to raise some qe stions on how journalism could or could not reinvent itself on the Internet, how independence was negotiated on the Net, at what price ().. I think there really was a utopian dimension in the beginning. And in any case, this is what I tell about in the film, that such utopian ideas have been caught up by

a ruthless reality to a large extent. This does not mean that what they do is not interesting, but that in any case they are obliged to compromise, to take into account an economic and technological reality. That is a real constraint, which is not the same as the economy of print. But it is no less real. ()..

From the perspective of a filmmaker, it was the innovativeness of *Rue89*, its core idea of making news free on the Internet, and its economic sustainability that made *Rue89* the most interestinge– ven compared to competing online projects. When listening to her speaking of the utopian dimension of *Rue89*, I was reminded of my time there, when I felt that I was in the midst of passion and ideals and life sacrifices for something bigger. This is also what made me remain with *Rue89* for a while and treat it like a window through which I could observe the world of entrepreneurial journalism. Even though the breakeven point was never reached, and journalistic innovations were criticized at times, the ideal of independence and the conviction that economic independence is necessary for editorial independence were key in keeping the organization togethert– ogether and functioning.

So, how do journalist-entrepreneurs "rely on the value of news to build profitable business models", which is a guarantee of independence? How are judgments of news worthiness and profitability reconciled in everyday and not-so-everyday work? This chapter addresses these qe stions on the basis of an extensive study of *Rue89*. I first tell the history of *Rue89* in different phases, highlighting the changes in the conciliation of news and profit. I then discuss different critical moments, when various forms of tension began to surface. Through this story, I show how the meaning of independence changed over time and how the process of testing and compromising around this principle unfolded.

THE BEGINNING: FROM NEWSPAPER JOURNALISTS TO ENTREPRENEURIAL JOURNALISTS

Former newspaper journalists started many of the entrepreneurial initiatives in journalism, especially in the first decade of the 2000s. In their study of online journalistic start-ups, Bruno and Nielsen (2012) examined 12 such cases in four European countries. When explaining their sample, they noticed the ambiguous relationship with the past, which was both embraced and rejected by the entrepreneurs:

> The cases we look at all have one foot in the past, in the sense that they consider themselves journalistic and they draw on the rich and diverse history and heritage of journalism. But they also have one foot in the future, drawing on new technologies that previous journalistic pioneers like Rudolf Augstein (the founder of *Spiegel*), Hubert Beuve-Méry (the first publisher of *Le Monde*), and Indro Montanelli

(long-term *Corriere della Sera* reporter and co-founder of *Il Giornale*) could not even have imagined, tools that are yet to be fully integrated into how the profession is practiced. (Bruno & Nielsen, 2012, p. 4)

In Europe, established journalists that had worked in traditional media started these entrepreneurial journalistic ventures. The German *Netzeitung*, founded in 2000 by the Norwegian pioneer who also started the online news website, *Nettavisen*, recruited the former editor of the daily *Berliner Zeitung* as editor-in-chief. Well-known newspaper and TV journalists founded the Italian *Il Post*, *Linkiesta*, and *Lettera 43*, the Spanish *El Espanol* and *El Confidencial*, and Britain's *The Bureau of Investigative Journalism*, to name a few such ventures. What Bruno and Nielsen (2012) called the *Nouvelle Vague* of online journalism—*Mediapart*— as founded not merely by the French newcomers; there were many established French journalists involved. Journalists from *Le Monde* and *Libération* founded *Mediapart*, a famous TV journalist founded *Arête sur Image*, and *Owni* and *Bakchich* had a significant number of experienced journalists in their newsrooms. *Rue89* was no exception; four of its five founders had long worked at *Libération*, which had been founded as a left-wing newspaper in 1973 by a group of French intellectuals, among whom was Jean-Paul Sartre. By the second half of the 1970s, the newspaper had already shifted to a more center-left or social-democratic position and abandoned the radical left ideas of its beginnings. During the 1980s and the 1990s, it grew significantly, changed ownership, and then, like many other traditional newspapers, experienced a crisis at the beginning of the 2000s. One of the recognizable characteristics of *Libération*popul   arly known as *Libé*—is its covers, which are image-based and often feature wordplay in a title.

As they usually told in the story of their origins, three of the *Rue89* founders had been bloggers from China, Washington, and New York, and they had realized through blogging that there were active readers on the other side of the screen. As one of them explained the first time we[3] met:

> While blogging as foreign correspondents, we discovered a new relationship with our readers. We developed a relationship through the comments that seemed to us to be enriching and useful for our work as journalists. It's a very different relationship from the one we had had with the readers until then. We told ourselves that the Internet, if well used, could be an instrument for re-establishing the trust link with readers. It seemed to us that a necessary condition was that the media develop something useful for people. (Interview with Gabriel, December 2011)

---

[3]   When I use "we" or "us" when speaking of the fieldwork, I refer to interviews that I conducted with Professor Pablo Boczkowski from Northwestern University.

With this discovery in mind, and while still living abroad as a foreign correspondent, Jules started thinking a new way of producing news: by drawing three circles on paper, which would later become the "Information with three voices", and by discussing this idea with several people in order to gain their support. Another founder remembered meeting Gabriel in New York in the autumn of 2006:

> We started discussing with Gabriel, who told me: "It is qi te funny because with Jules and Dominiqe , we are thinking about leaving *Libération* ().. ", because they had in mind to create a 100% Internet media company. And I told myself: "This is my opportunity." Because I was passionate about the idea of using the Internet for producing news in a new way. ().. So, we met a second time, and we said that we needed to go deeper into this. We opened a space for discussion online. It was called *projet Cerise.* ().. The idea was to create a hybrid newspaper with contributions from readers, users, and journalists. (Interview with Cezanne, June 2011)

When the three correspondents were back in Paris at the end of 2006, they knew that *Libération* was in crisis, and they presented their project to the management of the newspaper. Their idea was that it would revolutionize *Libé*'s news production and its organization:

> Well they had difficulties [at *Libé*], which I understand because I could do this only after I had cut the cord with *Libé*. They had many difficulties, and it's the case for all the newspaper companies today to understand that their main product is the daily newspaper, which corresponds today to 80% of their revenues. [It] needs to change, to be qe stioned, and perhaps it needs to be even secondary. When I was leaving *Libé*, I told this to the leading editor, and he asked me: "What can I do to keep you here?" I told him "Only one thing could keep mei— f you reverse the proportions [the relationship between newspaper and website]. You make the website the admiral ship and you make a paper supplement." I told him, "If you put the newsroom energy on the website, you'll make the most beautiful website in the world. There is no website that will have such a beautiful newsroom as the one we can offer with 70 journalists." He told me: "You're totally crazy." He was right, because it wasn't possible. It isn't possible to shift from one day to the other in this way. ().. he was totally right, but I think that his reaction showed how attached he was to the heavy structure that is *Libération*. It is primarily a newspaper, and the website is a small supplement thatone hopesw- ill bring some money. (Interview with Jules, December 2011)

Thus, the three correspondents enrolled another editor onto their project, and all four left *Libé*. Their idea was to make a participatory website for qa lity news. As one of them told us, some of their fellow journalists considered the idea of participation at the launch of the website as a betrayal to journalism.

The departure of four experienced journalists from an established newspaper did not pass unnoticed by the rest of the press, and their new project started receiving media attention even before the website was launched. In this way, many young journalists became interested and asked to participate in the project. A standing joke at *Rue89* is the story of one of the founders being approached on the street close to home by a teenager who had read about the project in the press, had just finished high school, and was interested in journalism. Having seen the *Rue89* founder on the street, the teenager asked about the project, was invited to Tuesday's meeting at Café Crème, ended up becoming a journalist, and worked for *Rue89* for seven years.

The founders' reputations from their time at *Libération* was useful for their new project, and even though they were breaking free of the newspaper to establish something new, their reputations followed them. They seemed to be aware of the legacy they carried from *Libération*—a reputation in both the journalists' professional community and in the general public:

> In fact, thanks to the Cécilia [Sarkozy] case[4] and thanks to the fact that we were a group of journalists coming out of *Libération*, we didn't need to prove who we were. We were a small group of people who had a professional legitimacy that was already recognized. And so, the fact that we continue this on another medium—that is, the Internet—seemed natural. Since we came out with one, two, or three pieces of information that were verified, and we haven't been qe stioned, we have been immediately recognized as a legitimate source, and we are regularly cited by *Le Monde*, the radio, etc. And this has surprised us—at least the speed with which it has happened. (Interview with Jules, December 2011)

The legacy of *Libération* was clearly recognized by the new entrepreneurs, who saw that their well-known past, often qualifying them as former *Libération* journalists, allowed *Rue89* to acqi re legitimacy qi ckly in a traditional journalistic senset—o be "recognized as a legitimate source" by the established media. The relationship with traditional media was thus ambiguous, as Bruno and Nielsen (2012) admitted. On the one hand, independence was loaded with new meaning against big media corporationst—he "entrepreneurial age" against the "institutional one", as *Politico*'s editors referred to it in their mission statement. On the other hand, experience in those corporations created continuity in practice and the sanctioning of "pure players" as legitimate sources of information by the traditional mediaa—t least in part.

To leave their established media companies reqi red these journalists to move outside their organizational boundaries. Practically, this meant finding new ways, new spaces, and new teams for working. The entrepreneurs had

---

[4]   On 6 May 2007t—he day of the *Rue89* launch and the day of the second round of the presidential election in France—*Rue89* published what they called a double scoop: the news that Cécilia Sarkozy did not vote for her former husband, Nicholas Sarkozy, and the news that the weekly newspaper *Le Journal du Dimanche*, which was aware of this information, decided not to publish it.

to reinvent their day-to-day work outside the central newsrooms and without access to such resources as Wi-Fi, printers and software. The story of the beginnings of the new journalistic enterprises echoes the mythology of some of the Internet giants. The garage in which Larry Page and Sergey Brin started Google and the garage in which Steve Jobs and Steve Wozniak launched Apple carry rich symbolism for many contemporary Internet entrepreneurs in many sectors of society. The garage becomes an innovation laboratory, with the low-cost, revolutionary potential permitted by the Internet. At *Rue89*, I soon heard about the Tuesday meetings at Café Crème, where many young journalists were invited and enrolled into the project. There was also the myth-ical kitchen of one of the founders— he place, like Page's and Brin's garages, where everything started. Over time, being in that kitchen became a symbol of belonging to the initial guard— he group that started the revolution. I noticed at my arrival at *Rue89* that the journalists were keen on informing when each person had arrived at *Rue89* and was therefore entitled to tell me the true story of Pierre's kitchen. Here is how Gervaise, one of the young journalists, told the story:

> Among people who were there at the very beginning, there were the four founders; I myself came right after them. Then, there were Noa and Marley, who came some weeks after me. Loan arrived, I think, one month after the launch and Yaël too. Yaël [who is technical staff] was actually in quite qi ckly a— week after the launch, or perhaps even before that. The first three, four months before the launch, many people were turning around. I arrived at the same time as others, and we had qi te a few meetings. We were about 15 people. One or two are remaining; the others left. The group was formed in this way. I think we must have been a dozen already at the start. Or perhaps around 10. At the beginning, we were a very small team, so it was very intense. We then organized ourselves. People took up their positions according to their competencies and their desires. (Interview with Gervaise, February 2011)

This account of who was there at the beginning and who came first and second illustrates the importance of the initial experience of *Rue89* in forming the group. As a senior editor, Dominiqe , told me in a conversation:

> Elena: I believe there are many traces of the beginning.
> Dominiqe : Yes, even among the journalists, it has created a sort of tacit hierarchy between those who had gotten to know each other in Pierre's kitchen and those who arrived after that. For example, I don't know if you have interviewed them, Francois and Sophie. I think that in their integration process, they have suffered for not being considered "true" [*Rue89*-ers] because they were not in the kitchen. (Interview with Dominiqe , June 2011)

The kitchen seems to have framed the beginnings of the project, located as it was between private and public, between hobby and job, between family and friends on the one hand and colleagues on the other. The beginnings were also narrated in a blog called *Le blog du making of*, in which selected stories about behind-the-scenes production were narrated and publicized. The blog attracted a few hundred readers and allowed them to come in direct contact with those who sat in the kitchen. It also created a sense of belonging, participating, and owning of what would develop into *Rue89*—not only among the initial journalists, but also among readers.

Le blog du making of was maintained as one of the website's blogs for several years. It was the place where the founders and some other journalists presented new products, discussed editorial and management decisions, and publicized the annual income statements. Like all the other articles on *Rue89*, the blog posts were open to comments. In time, this blog became a privileged discussion forum about the editorial, economic, and organizational "making of *Rue89*".

Gervaise described how the initial "*Rue89* spirit" became transformed over the years as the organization grew and employed more people:

> In the beginning, … it was really flat. There was really the start-up side, where you didn't really make a border between your private life and your job, so we have imposed some limits to ourselves [since then]. (Interview with Gervaise, February 2011)

The initial phase of "flexible organizing" depended on friendships among *Rue89* members rather than the usual professional relationships. Claude, one of the older journalists, reflected in an interview on the difficulties of transforming the initial project group into a regular work organization:

> It's normal that there are these tensions at the moment of passage from the start-up status to that of the real enterprise, in which we can no longer be happy with managing people through an emotional relationship. It was necessary to put things on the table, to clarify the rules of the game.
> … The difficulty was that there was a mix of work and friendship relationships between qi te a few journalists and that the border is very wobbly. It's very good that we aren't managed like a normal media company, and we're not large enough to be able to afford that, but it is qi te a mess, especially financially. (Interview with Claude, May 2011)

THE NEW WEBSITE

The founders promoted *Rue89* as what they called the "information revolution", and they insisted that their attempt would create a new kind of journalism. At the launch of the website, *Le Monde* announced *Rue89* in an article entitled "Old *Libération* journalists create a new news website" (Santi, 2007) and reported on the founders' intentions to "'marry professional journalism and participatory culture of the Internet' and situate itself between traditional news website and the blogosphere" (Santi, 2007).

The name *Rue89* was to signal the information revolution they wanted to orchestrate. The initial working name of the project was *Cérise* (cherry), as a designer, Leone, recalled in an interview:

> But Cérise was a weak name. We needed to find a funkier name—a little more swing. So we started brainstorming and thought about Rue66 and then Rue68. Then Jules said: "We invert it: *Rue89*." And everybody liked it. After all, the name is extremely important.(. Interview with Leone, July 2011)

Then, some of the founders sat together for 15 days, designed the website, and put it in place technically. Even if the design was qi te simple, there were a few details that were difficult to manage, as the designers decided to use a new, open access software, called *Drupal*.

The founders' experiences as former bloggers at *Libération* informed the way in which the website was designed. From the beginning, they thought that readers would be involved in the production cycle and that articles would roll out in chronological order, because the basic structure of website was initially qi te similar to that of a blog. The visual design of the website had been critical from the beginning. Leone lamented about the general negligence of design and form in France:

> In France people are qi te intellectual compared to the Anglo Saxons. At that time, I was in conflict with *Libération* because therea— nd it is a little bit the case even of *Rue89*, though less than *Libération*t— he journalists want to be writers. That's their dream. They don't care about the form. It's the text that's important.

Leone's goal with *Rue89* design was to give the impression of a comprehensive website where things were happening, in order to provide the reader with a picture of a complex world. The layout had three main columns:

(1)   a central column, with most of the articles rolling chronologically, except for the first and second position;[5]

---

[5]   The first position was the opening of the website. The picture accompanying this position was always bigger than the pictures in the following positions and was to be interpreted as the most important news that *Rue89* was publishing at that time. The second position just below the first was called "PDLP" internallya— n acronym for *"place de la pute"*t— he place for news that was considered funny, challenging, and/or a uniqe fit for the *Rue89* spirit.

(2)   a right-hand column, the opinion and debate space, with the heading, *"L'info à trois voix"*, in which three article titles hint at the co-production of content by journalists, experts, and readers;

(3)   a left-hand column, with promotional content for *Rue89*, like the micro-advertisement wall, plus the information about the company.

The use of the left-hand column changed over time. I observed more than once that that space had become the place for articles that were not well written and for which newsroom members were unsure about readers' reception. It was often a temporary placement for articles with uncertain qa lity and which could later on be transferred to the central column.

The website was then organized in *rubriques* (sections) constructed as tag pages[6] under the heading *Rue89*. There were eight sections under the heading *Rubriques* in the navigation bar at the top of the website: world, politics, society, ecology, hi-tech, media, culture, and sports. In September 2008, *Rue89* started a separate sub-website to report on economic issues. It was called *Eco89* and constituted a website within *Rue89*'s content management system. It had a different URL, because it was thought that a separate brand on economic issues would attract advertising. *Eco89* has not really taken off, however; it has never been recognized as an entity separate from *Rue89*.

MAKING A NEW JOURNALISM

Rue89 was created as a website of news and debate, co-produced by jour-nalists, users, and experts. This was a new kind of journalism when Gabriel, Dominiqe , and Jules launched it, but not the only novelty I found at *Rue89*. The lightness and inclusiveness of the organizational culture really surprised me.

I arrived at *Rue 89* with some anxiety, preoccupied about finding my place at the right distance from my interlocutors and about managing the relationship with the bosses in a better way than I had done in my earlier study (Raviola, 2010). But as soon as I walked through the door of *Rue89* and met some of the young and old journalists, the atmosphere of fun and dedication that dominated *Rue89* completely absorbed me. The news conferences I had assisted at in established newspapers looked more like a series of "shopping lists", as jour-nalists themselves put it, but at *Rue89*, journalists were continually discussing

---

[6]   Articles are given several tags (keywords), and the content management system gathers all the articles with the same keyword when it is searched in the website's search engine or when the URL www.rue89.com/keyword is typed.

and confronting each other with every possible idea, big and small. And there was lots of laugher. As Marley told me the first time we met:

> ().. one thing is clear at *Rue89*. There is an editorial freedom absolutely unheard of. In particular, Dominiqe and Jules, but also Gabriel, are really excellent, excellent journalists... Dominiqe , was one of my role models before I got to know him. I read him on *Libé*. Jules has become so since ().. . But those people are anyhow among the best of their generation, and it's really a pleasure to work with such talented people. So good. (Interview with Marley, March 2011)

Many of the journalists mentioned freedom as the distinctive feature of working at *Rue89*. During my time in the newsroom, I could observe how freedom was realized in relation to the interests, ideas, and self-managed time of each journalist, the perceived necessities of the website, and the control exercised by the chief editors.[7]

In this section, I describe the new journalism of *Rue89* under four key labels: participatory journalism, "feel like", angle, and humor.

Participatory Journalism

Through blogging, the founders had discovered the possibility of a new relationship with readers, and they wanted to change the news world by inviting non-journalists into the news production cycle. "Participation" became a keyword of the *Rue89* project, which the founders always tried to defend, although practices of co-production changed along the way and were not without frictionsbot h internal and external. When in New York, Gabriel thought up a model with the three intersecting voicest— he journalists, the users, and the expertsa— nd it quickly acqi red a hierarchical structure. As their handbook states, "*Rue89* is a 'three-voiced' site, but it is the first one that sets the tone." The first voice is the journalists,' which should keep the key, in order to control and guarantee a certain qa lity of news. *Rue89* developed as "a journalistic medium", as one of the founders called it during a public interview (Jesuisunclown, 2010). Behind it was the explicit intention to be faithful to basic journalistic principles and practices, but this did not mean an exclusive participation of journalists in news production. The readers rapidly

---

7   In this chapter, I refer to the leading editorial team of the newsroom as "chief editors", which included the three founders and the vice-chief editor of the newsroom. The three founders had the formal titles of president, general manager, and editor-in-chief, but they all assumed editorial responsibilities at times. I use the generic term "chief editors" to strengthen my interlocutors' anonymity.

and clearly took a central role on the website. As another founder explained in the same interview:

> Since the first day, we realized that we were doing something very different in terms of journalism. The day we launched the website online, we saw the users writing comments, appropriating the website, and we felt that we were creating a medium that did not totally belong to us. It is true that it's a journalistic medium with a newsroom, but it is a medium that's shared with our users, and the way we work is very different from the way we had been working earlier in the traditional medium. And we have felt this since the first day, when we put the platform on the sea, so to speak. (Jesuisunclown, 2010)

The revolution that *Rue89* stood for was driven by the desire to dismantle the closed boundaries of journalism and make it more open, accessible, and transparent to readers, experts, and everybody else, while simultaneously upholding the principles of journalism. The participation of readers, through comments, co-written articles, and other forms, was a central practice in this revolution, but so were traditional journalistic practices.

Although *Rue89* was the French pioneer in involving readers in journalistic news production, this idea was not new and became even more common after the launch of *Rue89*. Uniqe to *Rue89* was the fact that participation was a central practice in news production, which had conseqe nces for the organization of the newswork. Although many other news organizations outsourced the moderation of comments or simply disregarded them, the *Rue89* journalists seriously tried to integrate reader participation in the daily work of journalists. Comments were just one way of doing this. Participation was practiced in various ways and gave rise to various formats for readers' engagement: comments, reader-written articles, and chats, for example. Readers could write *comments* on every article on the website, and they were published automatically without a priori moderation. Readers could also write entire *articles*, spontaneously or in response to a journalist's suggestion, and these articles were subjected to the scrutiny of the newsroom. Readers could also participate in the Thursday news meeting through a *live chat*.

What Do You Feel Like Doing?

For a journalist to "feel like doing something specific" was a key dimension of organizing the news production at *Rue89*. In the news conference, rather than ordering journalists to write certain pieces, the editors would distribute work on the basis of the journalists' interests, by asking the simple q estion: "Who feels like doing X?" Or sometimes, more directly: "Sara, do you feel like dealing with it?" In response, when journalists were proposing their pieces, they felt free to say that they felt like doing something as justification for their choice.

As one journalist so described: "[The way you prioritize your work] is going to be a mix between what the editor feels you like to be doing and your own feelings" (Interview with Maxime, March 2011). "Feeling like doing it" has become an irrefutable justification for covering or not covering certain news, although it was negotiated collectively. As Maxime eloqe ntly described later, working at *Rue89* contributes to a collective feeling for doing some things and not othersa— feeling that arises by considering journalists' individual interests, the bosses' preferences, and the editorial needs of the website.

Angle

The angle was another key concept that shaped the notion of "feeling like doing this and not that". As the internal handbook for *Rue89* journalists explained (p. 1), "[t]he angle is sacred at Rue89". At Rue89, the most sacred trick after Champagne Marcoult and the disco ball in the third office of Rue89 is for journalists to know if they "hold the angle". To do so, they ask three qe stions:

1. How many essential ideas does my potential article contain? (If the answer is more than one, give up.)
2. Could I summarize what I mean in one short sentence?
3. If I read this to my neighbors, will they yawn or widen their eyes?

The angle is the uniqe twist in the news coverage and what journalists continuously search for in framing their pieces. In the news conference, I often heard an editor or a journalist asking another journalist: "What's the angle?" and then adding to an unconvincing answer: "If we don't have an angle, we don't do it." The obsession with the angle is in line with the desire of *Rue89* to innovate and offer something new to the public, different from the traditional press.

The insistence on the angle is justified not only in journalistic terms, but also in economic and organizational terms. *Rue89* does not subscribe to news agency services, which are deemed too expensive in relation to their contribution, and thus the journalists have access to the general news only through the dispatches of other media publishing agencies. The founders have argued that this is a cost-saving measure that also forces the journalists to find their own original angles to the news and provide uniqe ness to the website.

The never-ending search for the right angle is also framed as a way of covering a great deal of news with few resources. The journalists and editors often mentioned the angle as their way of being present for certain news in an interesting way, despite the difficulty of traveling and reporting, the overload of work forcing people to work on "36 articles at a time", as Stéphane told me, and the lack of specialized competencies on a specific theme. As Anaël, one of the editors, explained, the choice of covering the Cannes Film Festival from the angle of comparing a premium and a low-cost budget of a festival visitor was a pragmatic choice:

> I have commissioned the piece to a freelancer. It will be on the website just before the Festival. I don't know if you have met Sam and talked about the culture section, because it is difficult for us to do cultural critiqe . We would need expertise. We don't have the means. So we remain on the practical stuff [of the Festival], which interests everybody and to which we can return during the whole Festival. (Interview with Anaël, April 2011)

Thus the angle worked as a trick to serve both editorial and management considerations: The right angle allowed *Rue89* to make good journalism by producing relevant and uniqe   news pieces, while keeping production costs under control.

Humor

The sound of laughter is my strongest memory of *Rue89*. Adjectives like "amusing", "funny", and "comical" were perfectly legitimate ways to judge news and could even help in the never-ending search and evaluation of the angle. Some news is even created with the pure intent of amusing the public or making fun of the establishment.

Apart from the traditional April Fool's jokes, another example beautifully illustrates the sense of humor exhibited at *Rue89*. At the beginning of April 2011, Frédéric Lefebvre, a French center-right politician active in then Sarkozy's Union for a Popular Movement was asked in an interview about his favorite book. He answered: "For sure, *Zadig et Voltaire*. Because it is a life lesson, and I plunge myself into it qi te often." Many readers and journalists pointed to the fact that the politician had confused the name of a literary work, *Zadig ou la Destinée* with the name of the author, resulting in *Zadig et Voltaire*. After discussing this event in the news conference, editors and journalists at *Rue89* decided to draw on the irony of the mistake and launch a Twitter game, encouraging people to come up with similarly funny slips. They created the hashtag #i bliolefebvre, which became a trendsetter within a couple of days. Other media wrote about the buzz, resulting in great laughs and a certain degree of satisfaction over their mischief-filled *Rue89* newsroom.

During my time at *Rue89*, I noticed that it was not only the journalists at *Rue89* who wanted to have fun; it was also the readers. Although joking was a normal and perhaps the most practiced way of writing comments, some of the readers I talked to accused *Rue89* of not tolerating their jokes. In fact, some of the readers saw their comments deleted and their accounts blocked because the newsroom decided that they did not respect the Comments Charter—a— set of ethical and legal rules to be respected in the comments. These readers disputed this judgment and saw it as intolerance for jokes.

PRACTICAL CHALLENGES IN CREATING THE NEW JOURNALISM

One of the editors used to talk about journalism at *Rue89* as a PORSCHE, an acronym for Participatory, Open, Reactive, Serendipitous, Collective, Humorous, and Enqi ring. These seven aspects of the PORSCHE did not always co-exist in a frictionless way, as they could imply different priorities in everyday work in the newsroom. This section is therefore about the everyday dilemmas recognized by journalists in the newsroom as part of their daily job, in three main areas: participation, short vs. long writing, and reactive vs. investigative articles.

Participation

Although participation was one of the key concepts at *Rue89*, participatory journalism revealed itself to be challenging at times. The general reqi rement for journalists working at *Rue89* was that everyone should engage in work with the readers, as the readers were *Rue89*'s sensors and sources. One of the most prominent methods of engagement was to read and moderate comments to the articles. As the *Handbook for Rue89 Journalists* said, "the thread of the comments is for [a *Rue89* journalist] a gold-bearing river" that the journalist "passes through a sieve in search of ideas and information".

Two examples of successful participatory journalism were often cited, both of them republished in the December 2010 magazine issue among the "Best of 2010". The first one was presented to my co-interviewer, Pablo, and me by Jules as "probably the best of the year for us" in December 2010:

> It was in August when real news was dead. We received through the contact mailbox a text from a young Moroccan engineer, graduated from one of the best schools in France and working here [in France]. It was in the middle of Sarkozy's campaign against foreigners, Roma people, his big speech, and so on. There were really bad vibrations about racism and xenophobia. And this guy sends this text, saying, "Maybe you won't even read it, but I wanted to express myself and to say that I have taken the decision not to stay in France. I'm going back to Morocco. I can't stand it anymore, this racist environment. I know it will be tough for me in Morocco, but at least it's my home and I prefer the struggle there than here." It was very articulate, very well written, and pointing at the right things. I found it too good to be true, so I called the guy. I met him; I checked everything about what he was saying, because he wanted me to put only his first name, as he was still working for a big company here in France. He wanted to finish the project before leaving. In the end, I was sat-

isfied with the text, and we published it. It created an amazing storm. It had almost 200,000 readings. This is a great deal for a text that is not going on Googlej— ust on social networks and in mass circulation. It had more than 2,000 comments. [When I checked in September 2017, 1,456 comments had been published]. So three days later, I took those 2,000 comments, and spend three hours reading every comment, and analyzing them. There were two or three points coming out. I published the analysis, which got 80,000 readings, and another 1,000 comments. [When I checked in September 2017, 567 had been published]. Suddenly, I received another text, written from a different perspective. The first guy was a Moroccan and a non-religious Muslim. The second guy said: "Okay, I'm French, born in Paris, and I'm religious and Muslim, and I want to be respected for what I am. I'm not leaving that place and fuck you." He was very brutal, but he was also an engineer like the first guy, and that's why he replied to the first guy. And he was a bit aggressive to the first guy: "You're flying and leaving, I'm staying and fighting, I want to be respected." He gave his name, so I had an exchange with him, and we published the second text, with the same ratio [of clicks and comments]: 200,000 readings, 2,000 comments! Then I received a third text, from a French-born man of French background, who was gay and agnostic. He said he had no problems with the first two guys, but he also wanted to be respected for what he was: "I'm also a part of French society and I don't feel much respect in France." And these three texts got 500,000 readings, and 5,000 commentsa— ll this in the middle of the summer [when we would expect fewer responses]a— really full debate on the one of the most complicated issue in French society today. (Interview with Jules, December 2011)

The founder realized that this is what *Rue89* should be aiming at: generating and then checking and organizing the debates. After all, no one (but a devoted editor) will read 2,000 comments. A 600-word summary is needed, pointing out the main aspects of the debate. In this way, even more comments, debates, and contributions are generated, which can then be published. On that occasion, they did the six pages with the three texts and an analysis of the comments.

Sam, another journalist, described a second example, which was also included in the *Best of 2010*:

Two young girls called me this summer, telling me they had a video project. In the video, they would be disguised with niqab tops, the full veil, like a burka though it is not the right word, and mini-skirts. They made a video in all the beautiful neigh-borhoods where the ministerial offices are located. I said: "Make the video and we'll see. But I want a text to accompany the video, explaining your approach, why you are doing thist— hat it is not just a provocation." If, on the other hand, I had gone to interview these girls, saying: "Hello, I've heard that you have such an idea…", they would take less responsibility for their act; they would say hardly anything. Instead, they made their video and wrote their text. It's not a manifesto; it's not at all pretentious; but thanks to it, we offered people the opportunity to take a stand. And for me it feels like I've done my job by carrying that stand, that point of view. After we published it, *Aljazeera* republished it.(. Interview with Sam, December 2011)

Practicing participatory journalism, however, did not always produce such virtuous examples. In everyday work, the combination of participatory and other journalistic practices produced at least three types of friction: time, value, and visibility and recognition.

Time: Many of the journalists I interviewed noted *the aspect* of time as a source of friction. All the journalists at *Rue89* were reqi red to moderate comments to their own articles, which meant that the publication of an article did not end the work of the journalist who wrote it. This extra responsibility reqi red a great deal of time and was perceived as diverting the journalists from their investigations. Journalists needed to read and moderate the comments, to engage in electronic conversations with readers via e-mail, and eventually to accompany them in the writing process. Editors needed to edit blogs written by non-journalists. Chief editors needed to give the non-journalistic contributions a position on the website.

I asked the journalists how much time they spent moderating the comments, and the usual answer was that it varied depending on the type of article published and its subject. As Marley explained:

> In fact, I have invented some words here, in the *Rue89* jargon. "Clickogenic". It's a subject that's going to generate a lot of views, to be read a lot. "Debatogenic" is something that's going to generate a lot of comments. With a very debatogenic subject, there will be many comments, so you'll have to spend a great deal of time on it.
>
> But on average, after the publication of an article, you spend one hour [moderating the comments] … In total, you spend around two hours [for each article], because the comments are open for four days. (Interview with Marley, March 2011)

Value: Journalists also mentioned *the aspect of value* as a source of friction. Several journalists considered participation as one of the strengths of *Rue89*, and some of them assigned participation an ideological value. Sam, who worked intensely with participation and who joined *Rue89* in its early days, told me explicitly that "It's qi te a political action, to make people feel authorized to speak, to write, to tell, to talk wherever they are" (Interview with Sam, March 2011).

Others considered participation valuable in helping journalists find information and cover areas that are geographically distant or focus on topics on which they have little expertise. As Jules explained:

> It's the most participative website possible in comments and testimonies [of readers writing about their own experiences]. We can activate a base of people to write for us very qi ckly. When we write about Tunisia, Egypt, Libya… we could easily activate people to testify ().. . Nobody has reached this level of interaction with the readers before. (Interview with Jules, December 2011)

The practical value of the comments was also recognized as helping to check the correctness of the information published on the website. Several of my interlocutors recognized the positive contribution of readers signaling factual errors and thus helping journalists to be even better and more precise at their job. As Yannick, a journalist, told me: "When we write an article and there's an error in it, someone would notice it and tell us̶e̶ nerally within five minutes. It's great." Stéphane, another journalist, confessed previous worries about being confronted with the audience responses:

> At the beginning it's almost scary. You tell yourself, "I'm going to show myself naked, and they will criticize me." Then you realize that it's great, because as soon as you do something stupid in your article, make an error with a figure, a date, a name, there will always be somebody who will qi ckly remark on it.
> Working with the comments is really very engaging, but also very tiring, because you do the job of three journalists at the same time, so you work much more... (Interview with Stéphane, February 2011)

Although the journalists recognized the value of participation, they also qe stioned its emotional conseqe nces for the authors and the qa lity of the contributions received. As Marley said:

> It's up to us to make the triage, and then it's up to us at times to understand the aspi-rations of the Internet userst̶ he why of a given reaction. Have we really done our job badly on that subject? And then, also, one has to watch out not to be subjected to the tyranny of the minority. It's 1% of the readers of *Rue89* who send comments, and sometimes we're very upset by three negative comments that come one after the other, but in fact it is 3 comments out of 200, and then when we reflect on it, we may find that they were wrong. Even if 3 out of 200 are saying the same thing, it's not much, and it's necessary to be able to resist. We can answer, we can debate with them and say: "We don't agree for this and this reason." Otherwisew. ell, there are contradictory comments; there are many opinions, and we can't give up our editorial line. Because if not, we will be subjected to a tyranny of the minority... it is like a politician who acts according to the polls. (Interview with Marley, March 2011)

Some of *Rue89*'s personnel lamented the progressive deterioration of partici-pation, especially in the comments. Yannick was qi te disillusioned:

> How do I manage the comments today? I do like everybody else; I moderate the articles and I really do force myself to respond as much as I can. To be very honest, I'm a little bit irritated by this. Because I find the qa lity of the comments on *Rue89* to be decreasing. I think there's an enormous number of idiots who let themselves go without having anything to say. It will be a relief when I leave *Rue89*. (Interview with Yannick, June 2011)

This phenomenon is not uniqe to *Rue89*: The increasing number and aggres-siveness of Internet trolls truly affected journalistic work at *Rue89*. Trolls were a recurrent topic of discussion, and the value of the comments was increasingly qe stioned.

Visibility and recognition: Yet another aspect raised by the journalists with regard to participatory journalism was *the question of visibility and recognition.* Coaching readers in writing their testimonies, editing a blog post, or engaging in an e-mail conversation with readers were all invisible tasks, which contributed to building the community of readers and commentators[8] around *Rue89*, but did not provide journalists with public recognition. As one of the journalists put it, the role of the journalist was transformed to that of an orchestra director rather than a soloist.

I did sometimes observe a qe stioning of the value of readers' certain contributions. Once a journalist published a testimony by a reader with who had contacted *Rue89* several times and who had written about the accidental distribution of a secret human resource file in his company. This contribution was positioned by the chief editors as the banner headline for the day and received 230,000 clicks. As Yannick said:

> It's huge. It has circulated enormously on Twitter, Facebook, on Internet. It has been linked a lot by other websites, because it's funny. As to the journalistic value of this piece of information, I am the first to say that it is qi te weak, but it is funny. It does extremely well on the Internet, as it's a light thing. (Interview with Yannick, June 2011)

During my visit to *Rue89* in 2011 and 2012, I did not hear many complaints about non-journalist contributors stealing visibility from the journalists. This had changed, however, when I returned at the beginning of 2017. By then, some of the editors were lamenting that the young journalists had gotten increasingly tired and resistant to the participatory work, and more specifically to the moderation of comments, because this work was invisible. "You cannot write your byline when you engage with the community", said one of the editors in an interview in January 2017, and thus young journalists thought it was not as worthy of merit as investigating and reporting.

Writing Long and Short

Finding a balance between long and short texts was recognized by many journalists as one of the main challenges in everyday work. The issue was discussed in meetings and in daily work and often came up during my interviews.

---

[8] Commentators were readers registered on the website who were allowed to comment on the articles.

Gervaise who had been at *Rue89* since the early days had what was perhaps one of the clearest explanations of how this tension arose:

> It is the eternal problem of treating the hot current news rapidly, effectively, while simultaneously making our own investigations. When we do a job that takes time, we are less focused on current news that is visible on the website [in terms of fewer articles and less freqe ntly updated website]. The alternative would be to give up making more investigative articles… And I don't have the solution. We have already discussed the solution of having someone every day who would be focused on hot current news. But the hot current news on Mondays is politics, and if the political journalist is at the desk, the other person would do it less well. We have discussed many possible solutions… In terms of work organization, the qe stion is how we can manage to do both. Because we cannot do hot current news all the time either. Then, there are days when everything is going well: You arrive in the morning, you do a current news thing, you have a good idea that it takes two hours, and then you have the rest of the day to do what you wantyour own investigations, leave for a reportage, whatever… And then there are those days when this isn't possible. So, I don't know what a good way would be to reconcile the two. I think it's something typical of all the websites, because we're into a permanent flow of current news. The website needs to flow, but the feeling of wanting to do something longer is still there.I. don't have solutions. (Interview with Gervaise, February 2011)

One of the foundersD- ominiqe of ten complained that the website was weak on "the R of reactivity", on the ability to produce news qi ckly. This may not be surprising, because, although not always explicitly expressed, many of the journalists I met at *Rue89* seem to have had some sort of dream of shoe-leather reporting, as in-depth investigative journalism is sometimes calledw- earing out shoes from walking place to place to observe things and speak to people first-hand, rather than sitting indoors at a desk. As Gervaise told me:

> I discussed this with [Yannick], and we said that the website needs to be fed. We have the right to do long stuff, but if we do one long thing, it's good if we do a short thing at the same time. In that way, we are present, we publish, we do something. (Interview with Gervaise, April 2011)

Maxime saw short texts as a sort of tax the journalists had to pay for the functioning of the website, allowing them to do what they really wanted to dol— onger investigations. Then the journalist mentioned an example from the same week. On Monday, Maxime had written a text on a newly launched news website, which was completed in one day:

> I told myself, it's good, it's a small article, it'll be done in a day. And then I'll be able to do my reportage in the South without feeling guilty, because I will already have published a text at the beginning of the week. So, I'll not be under too much pressure. (Interview with Maxime, March 2011)

Different journalists judge and handle the problem of short vs. long texts differently. As Maxime remarked in another conversation:

> Already, we realize that [Journalist A] produces much less than [Journalist B, previously in the same position]. I think the texts are of better qa lity, but [Journalist A] produces less. So, I don't understand why we don't ask ourselves how we can replace the continuous flux of [Journalist B], even if we ought to keep [Journalist A], who does politics very well. (Interview with Maxime, June 2011)

Yannick talked about being mocked for being slow:

> At the beginning, you reason like a press journalist. You're going to tinker with your article so it will be perfect. But now it doesn't bother me any more to write articles where at the end you add a short sentence: "More information will follow." And you qi ckly publish the article that you fill in little by little. My bosses joke all the time because I'm very slow. Still, I go much faster now. (Interview with Yannick, June 2011)

The struggle between short and long texts signaled an unsolved tension: Doing qa lity journalism brings journalistic recognition and potentially creates readership but takes time from continuously feeding the website with material, which certainly brings audiences and clicks, and therefore advertising revenues. In a 2009 meeting with investors discussing *Rue89*'s strategy, one of the founders formulated this tension explicitly: "Every long reportage costs us a great deal, as we see the audience decreasing directly" (Management and steering committee meeting, spring 2009, video material collected but not used for the film, *La Rue est à eux*).

The balance between short and long texts was widely discussed, and the journalists considered it a significant factor in their daily work, particularly accentuated by the absence of deadlines in online news production. The newsroom was permanently in a wrapping-up phase. As Céleste put it:

> I have learnt lots of things here: to make videos, to be active on social mediaw ell, to be a real web journalist. What is most disturbing when one arrives in a newsroom… is the fact that there are no wrappings-up, there are no deadlines. The articles need to be published as qi ckly as possible as soon as they are ready. This changes the rhythm of work completely. (Interview with Céleste, March 2011)

Papers that are qi ckly written are called HuffPos, with reference to the participatory USA-based website *Huffington Post*. According to Marley, the *Huffington Post* publishes "very qi ck articles, which report information from somewhere else, make some paragraphs out of it, contextualizing it in a different way, changing the angle of the article. We do the same and we call them 'HuffPos', in our internal jargon."

Reactive and Investigative Journalism

The tension between short and long texts echoes the tension between cold and hot stories. Articles are hot when they deal with a current piece of news and must therefore be published as soon as possible. They are cold when they deal with long-term issues, and thus the value of their publication does not expire qi ckly. This type of article reqi res different working time and has a different relationship to the wider news agenda at a certain time.

The Internet, with its continuous publishing loop, seems to set new conditions for this relationship between hot and cold stories. Stéphane, having had experience from the print newspapers, expressed concerns in this regard:

> It's complicated... I've always done cold things, rather magazine-like subjects. I already have an investigation, a magazine-like thing that I am writing about. The qe stion is how we insert something hot. Do I have enough time for a small hot text, or should I be happy with a lookout? That's my internal debate every time, and it depends on the time, on the inspiration, and on the energy... (Interview with Stéphane, March 2011)

The balance between cold and hot subjects depends also on the area of coverage. For politics, mixing cold and hot subjects is more important than it usually is for environmental issues or media. This balance has implications for the way work is organized over the course of the day. Yannick, who is responsible for one of the website sections, explained:

> I like that in my sections I need to be less reactive, as they are colder sections. Conseqe ntly, there is a rhythm in my work, which is more convenient; if I were on hotter sections, I would have more pressure. (Interview with Yannick, February 2011)

THE ROUTE FROM THE KITCHEN TO THE NORMAL

The organization of work was an extensively debated issue at *Rue89*. This topic was also the link between editorial discussions on the kind of journalism practiced at *Rue89* and management choices on how to develop *Rue89* as a business and how to finance its operations. This issue was also identified as critical for the growth of *Rue89* and its path from a start-up to a "regular" news organization. In this section, I describe how work was organized in the newsroom, as it represented the primary compromise between the editorial and management worlds. In the next section, I discuss specific incidents during which this compromise was challenged.

In the beginning, *Rue89* was the main part of the journalists' life. This is how one of the founders described it:

> At first, three months before the launch and six months following the launch, I had to start at 8:00 AM and finish at 2:00 AM the next morning, something like that. Imagine, for nine months, eight months, or something like that. But all that time, people produced impeccable texts... there was this thing that is not anywhere else ().. in the press. For example, my people passed something that was happening on a street, and then they would use their video cameras, and they would call me at 1:00 AM, and we would put it online then. (Interview with Placide, May 2011)

As Placide described it, not without a certain degree of enthusiasm, at those times the boundaries between working and non-working time were extremely loose. In the beginning, *Rue89* played a key role in the life of many journalists, in terms of both time and engagement. This initial start-up feeling and the volunteer engagement lasted until early autumn of 2007. It was, in fact, only about four months after the launch that people started to be employed, as the first round of fundraising brought new capital into the company.

The continuous time flow, without deadlines and fixed working hours, started to create some problems, however. If this were to be a regular job, there was a need for a schedule. As a continuation of Tuesday's meeting at Café Crème, Thursday 9:00 AM meetings were introduced qi te early in the life of *Rue89* and became a central point in the organization of work. The meeting was called "Sitting reunion" and lasted between 60 and 90 minutes. All the journalists in the newsroom and between 1 and 6 interns were present at this meeting.

The meeting had three phases: First, the most important events to cover in the coming week were listed, with discussions among team members about if and how to cover them. Then the editor-in-chief read readers' suggestions from the live-blogged news conference of the previous week (as described later). Finally, everyone told what they were planning to do the next week. The order was determined by the seating order, which was not fixed, but often started with politics. This last phase was often the longest one.

During this meeting, the discussions were live-blogged by two editors. Using a tool called CoverItLivea– microblogging tool similar to Twitter— they discussed with readers who were connected to the meeting, and who gave feedback about the past week's coverage. There was a discussion of proposals of issues to be covered and suggestions for the articles that the editors would be writing about in the coming week. There were some 10 to 15 of these readers at any one time—often the same persons. The bloggers did not communicate all the subjects discussed during the meeting, as some of them were considered exclusive, so that the discussions in the room and on the live blog were parallel rather than overlapping. Sometimes the editors directly communicated with the rest of the journalists about the readers' comments on a certain topic under discussion.

Daily work at *Rue89* was structured around a short morning news meeting at 9:30 AM and a longer weekly news conference held on Thursdays between 9:00 AM and 10:30 AM (Raviola, 2017). During the short daily morning meeting all journalists briefly presented what they would be working on during the day, while the editors planned their work for the day. After this meeting, also called standing reunion, because all the participants were standing, the journalists went to their desks and started working on the articles they had been assigned. Through the so-called "morning battle", the newsroom worked towards the goal of publishing five new articles on the website before 1:30 PM. At that time, in fact, a daily automatic newsletter was sent to the registered readers. There were no other meetings during the day. Lunch was usually a time of conviviality, and many of the journalists took lunch break together, leaving only a few people to cover the newsroom. The end of the working day was around 7:00 or 8:00 PM.

The introduction of the morning meeting in the autumn of 2008 raised criticism from some of the younger journalists. They interpreted the meeting as a hindrance to their freedom and an intrusion on their liberty to decide what to do and when to do it. As Yannick explained to me:

> Yannick: It was introduced because everyone did what they liked…
> Elena: With regards to the use of time?
> Yannick: Yes. Coming at 9.30 or 11 AM if you're not an early bird, which I am not… Personally I was against it, because I like to sleep. Well, it is true, now we know when the day begins. This is clear. And then we're free to organize our own time. I have long subjects, investigations which I work on for several weeks. (Interview with Yannick, February 2011)

Yannick's words revealed traces of a past controversy between freedom ("doing what they liked") and efficiency and coordination ("knowing when the day begins"). In this controversy, the standing meeting was too much in one frame ("I was against") and necessary in the other ("This is clear"). It seems also that the situation cooled down and the freedom principle surrendered to efficiency: The meeting was accepted as appropriate and was performed every day.

As one of the editors—Claude—described, this acceptance did not happen spontaneously and without organizational memory: "There was a lot of resistance to it and it was taken like a sort of betrayal, like we had sold our souls. All this came out later on, in a meeting in 2010" (Interview with Claude, May 2011). This controversy was overcome thanks to a pragmatic compromise: The journalists agreed to attend the meeting without agreeing with its principle of worth.

As another journalist remembered, however, the atmosphere became particularly heated during one meeting in 2010. During a short period previous to this meeting, one of the editors had introduced a new management tool: an Excel sheet completed daily by one of the editors after the standing morning meeting; it comprised a list of what every journalist planned to work on each day. This Excel sheet was to be a control tool that helped to distribute the work among the journalists and plan the work of the editors, in accordance with the same principle of efficiency that justified the introduction of the standing meeting. The opposition to the Excel sheet was so strong and reactions to it so heated that the founders decided to give it up and go back to "a few notes written on an envelope", as Claude said (Raviola, 2017). As I observed (Raviola, 2019, p. 741): "The journalists at *Rue89* were simply not ready to reframe the Excel sheet as an appropriate tool not   for efficient coordination and control or for better and more creative journalistic work." When this became clear, the editor who introduced the tool decided to leave the organization, convinced that its management could not be professionalized.

Most of the journalists did not work in the newsroom on the weekend, although they often finished articles at home. Yet because the website was kept alive during the weekend, there were always at least three people working on Saturdays and two on Sundays. On Saturdays there were a journalist, a desk editor, and a chief editor, according to the rotation scheme. On Sundays there were a desk editor and a chief editor. As there were four chief editors, each of them worked at least one weekend per month. But there were only three desk editors, so they had to work one weekend out of three. For the six or seven journalists, the weekend work was less regular.

There were other regular appointments at *Rue89*: a general meeting on the first Friday of the month to discuss organizational issues and a general meeting on the third Friday of the month for some kind of training, according to current needs. Various discussions often developed on the staff e-mail among team members, along with announcements of parties and celebrations, which were qi te regular, often organized at the offices of *Rue89*, and included former members of the team and close friends of the team.

MOVING FORWARD: SHIFTING PEOPLE, ENGAGEMENT AND MONEY

Rue89 was born out of an entrepreneurial dream of revolutionizing journalism and realizing a new model of independence, through which money would be instrumental to newsmaking, and profit would be functional to the project of independence. The journey from a founder's kitchen to a "normal" enterprise was not without friction, and tensions emerged around the way different actions were deemed a worthy undertaking or an unworthy undertaking.

One of the crucial shifts in this journey was the shift in the modes of engagement in working at *Rue89*. Claude, an experienced journalist who joined *Rue89* a few months after its launch, described the transition in this way:

> ... rather than the launch, what I found fascinating in that period was the transition between a start-up and a normal enterprise. It was the turning point between the two. It was the fact that there could have been at the same time and in the same people both a nostalgia for the kitchen and the desire to be treated like all the other journalists, to have weeks of paid leave, reimbursed phone bills. What I found really interesting was the passage from one culture to the other and the fact of aspiring to be both at the same time. (Interview with Claude, June 2011)

In this q ote, Claude is describing the contradictions of making the *Rue89* project a normal enterprise, where people would be engaged in work like employees in other companies, rather than like friends triggering a revolution. Like an editor used to say, this transition was like that of a snake changing skin, and many early comers ended up leaving the organization as new ones entered and shaped the direction of normality. Claude told me about the moment that everything seemed to be shifting to "being a normal company":

> It is funny because ().. during the move to another office, one thing was highly symbolic for me, even if it was a small detail. [Gabriel and the secretary] had been at Ikea to buy stuff for the new office, and when they got back, among the things they brought back was a clock. I asked them: "Why have you bought a clock?" And they answered: "Well, because we wanted to." It was the first time we bought something we didn't really need, but, in my opinion, it was because normal companies have a clock. At that point I remembered when Gervaise went to buy a wastepaper basket and was looking at all the models to buy the cheapest one. For me, the purchase of that clock symbolized the transition into a more normal company. When the enterprise became more normal, which was also what we wanted, we began to have employees looking at the company, asking ourselves, "Could I be paid more somewhere else? Have better working conditions?" (Interview with Claude, June 2011)

In the process of transforming a start-up into a normal enterprise, the notion of worth was repeatedly translated, and eventually split into two conflicting ideas of worth. This development was openly criticized in the organization, although justifications for different critiques also varied. The two ways of practicing independence did not always work together without friction in daily organizing. Several critical moments succeeded one other, taking different forms, triggered by different events, and involving different people.

5. Reframing the new independence: making money for news?

The main compromise between journalism and management at *Rue89* could be expressed in the conviction that economic independence is needed as a guarantee of editorial independence. Thus, news was to be made and valued in ways that satisfied journalistic qa lity and simultaneously considered the financial constraints of the new enterprise. As one of the journalists said in our informal conversation, "At *Rue89*, everybody likes to theorize, to reflect on what will revolutionize journalism. But it's also necessary to be realistic about the means we have" (Conversation with Yannick, Fieldnotes, June 2011).

This chapter is about the tension between the desire to revolutionize journalism and the necessity of being realistic about the means at hand and how it played out in the development of *Rue89* as a journalistic enterprise. It is an analysis of specific incidents in which this tension became particularly visible.

BREAKEVEN AND ITS MYTHOLOGY

Initially, the *Rue89* business model was to provide free news to a wide audience and thereby attract advertisers to the website. Advertising revenues were to serve as the main source of income that would finance the main activity: news production. The founders and journalists of *Rue89* often discussed possible and viable economic models, looking for one that could guarantee a stable balance between revenues and costs and generate a profit. Economic independence was considered a reqi rement for editorial independence, as one of the minority shareholders (who owned about 3% in 2011) put it:

> As *Rue89* is not owned by the state and isn't an association, it needs to be financially profitable. It's the only way to be independent. So now it's necessary to find the way, beyond the ideals and all this, for the website to become independent, absolutely financially independent, in order to make the editorial line independent. (Interview with a minority shareholder, June 2011)

The public's right to be informed ("the ideals and all this") and the necessity of making a profit ("it needs to be financially profitable") are co-existing principles at *Rue89*, and they are both used to make people, things, and practices newsworthy. These two principles were often pitted against each other as they clashed in daily practice, and their order of priority was one of the employees' major concerns. *Rue89* attempted to reinvent independent journalism online by creating a composite situation that would permit it to respect different principles through daily and long-term pragmatic compromises.

In these daily pragmatic compromises, one issue seemed particularly significant at *Rue89*: "breakeven".[1] Breakeven was seen as an ideal compromise between the expenditures of journalism and the commercial gains it generateda— state of affairs that must be achieved in order to maintain independence and fulfill the promises of the *Rue89* project. Publishing the annual results for 2010 in a blog post, one of the founders identified two priorities for the future development of *Rue89*: "Continue to invest in technological and journalistic development and continue to move toward the economic balance, breakeven, which is the condition for maintaining our independence" (Mauriac, 2010).

The founder also insisted on the necessity of linking these two priorities, in order to ensure that an increase in costs due to technological and journalistic development corresponded to a proportional increase in revenues. As another founder explained during a strategy meeting,[2] this meant that only profitable projects and activities that guaranteed a revenue stream would be undertaken. There was also a persistent and general effort to decrease operating expenses as a way of reaching breakeven, in light of what many of the journalists called the "philosophy of the family father".[3]

Breakeven was often discussed not only among founders of *Rue89*, but also among employees and the commentators who wrote comments on the website. Commentators were members of the community who registered on the website, which enabled them to write comments on the articles. In *Rue89* language, they were called *riverains* (neighbors) of *Rue89*.

In my initial interviews with the people at *Rue89*, many of them talked about breakeven as an organizational goal for the year and about the importance of reaching it. This surprised me, as this issue did not arise in my earlier studies of newsrooms, and neither was it mentioned in the newsroom ethnographies I have read. Yet in this journalistic venture, discussions could rapidly shift

---

[1]   Breakeven is the point of economic balance in a businessm— aking neither profit nor loss—the point at which revenues and costs are eqa l.

[2]   During strategy meetings the founders and all employees discussed key qe stions about the future development of *Rue89*. These meetings were held from time to time, when the management of *Rue89* called them.

[3]   By "philosophy of the family father", they meant the desire and actions to save money by reducing costss— upposedly like the father does for his own family. It is noticeable that this philosophy is ascribed to the father, and not to the mother, as it would be in other languages.

from the news to be covered that day to the way the company could reach breakeven in the short and long term̶bot h in the name of independence.

One day I met one of the journalists, Gervaise, at a café. Gervaise had left *Rue89*, and as he told me:

> I knew the numbers by heart, I knew how much that would mean on a yearly basis and in relation to our cash, if we increased people's salaries by, let us say, 10%. I really had a clear view of the numbers, which is not at all the case at the organization where I work now. (Interview with Gervaise, June 2011)

Indeed, when I first arrived at *Rue89*, I was taken by the common awareness of the company's economic constraints and its accounts. Considering the ideals behind the launch of *Rue89*—like free news, participation, dismantling the corporatist barriers of journalism̶— was often inclined to think of *Rue89* as an ideological utopian society or some sort of social venture, but I was continuously reminded of the fact that this was a corporation. Everyone at *Rue89* agreed that the company needed to make money in order to guarantee its editorial independence.

Boltanski and Thévenoux's (2006) six "orders of worth (inspiration, market, industrial, domestic, fame, and civic)", discussed in greater detail in Chapter 1, are relevant here. In trying to reconcile editorial and management principles, the founders and the employees mixed a sense of civic worth̶— he public right to be informed—with three other orders of worth: market worth, fame worth, and a sense of industrial worth driven by efficiency and functionality. In fact, development in journalism means a bigger audience or greater readership, which both increases advertising revenues and fulfills the journalists' desires to be recognized. Independence is supposed to align all these principles of worth somehow, and *Rue89*, including its website, attempts to realize this goal with composite arrangements, proving (or sometimes failing to prove) the possibility of doing so. In practice, there were many discussions about what was worth doing and what was not.

In particular, there was growing concern about the inability of reaching breakeven and about the potential conseqe nces of that failure. The first time we were told the history of *Rue89*, Jules distinguished between two sides: "the journalist side and the business side" (Interview with Jules, December 2010). On the journalist side, things had gone as expected, or perhaps even better, as *Rue89* had become a well-known news website in a relatively short time. On the business side, however, things had been more difficult than expected, and although the possibility of reaching breakeven seemed to be close, it had yet to be realized. This view was shared by the other founders and journalists.

As this financial situation was well-known to everyone who worked at *Rue89*, they often discussed possible ways of keeping costs low. One way was to keep travel costs low. Stéphane, who had previously worked for a weekly newspaper, told me that "this frugality" seemed rewarding when being recruited, and that it seemed to be good for the organization to find new solutions. Only later came the realization that an organization that could not afford high salaries meant that there was less money for the private lives and leisure activities of its employees. At that point Stéphane realized that saving money for the organization implied a decrease in private savings, and decided to join the rest of the employed journalists in arguing for higher salaries.

Apart from interfering in the private sphere, the economic constraints are also "interiorized" by journalists in their newswork at *Rue89*. As Stéphane told me:

> Stéphane: I felt really bad the other week... I have followed [a famous politician], only two days, yes. I saw the money that I spent, and I said that if I were going to ask for such a significant reimbursement at [the publication where I was previously working], this would not have posed any problem...
> Elena: How much was it?
> Stéphane: I don't know, but some hundreds of euros. It was two flight tickets, a train ticket, a hotel night, and I told myself that during the campaign the other newsrooms would do this every day for months and months. But I thought it would be too expensive for us and I held myself back a little on the travel. I try to go when I think it's really worth it, but I know really in my heart that it's when we go and don't know what will happen or when we [think we're going] for nothing that things happen. There is the idea of ensuring the catch, of not going for nothing and I tell myself: "If it were worthless, would I dare not write the article?" I have asked myself this kind of qe stion. I do my reimbursements very differently than before. The custom is that you also put your meals there for your travel, and this time in fact I paid them myself. I told myself that even in Paris I would have paid myself. I try to help them make savings to my detriment, which is not good at all. (Interview with Stéphane, June 2011)

Stéphane's reasoning shows how intricate was the relationship between economic and journalistic considerations at *Rue89*. The worth of a journalistic effortt— raveling for a reportage or an investigationw— as judged not only on the basis of its news value, but also on the basis of its cost. The journalist even wondered about daring not to produce an article or feeling constrained about having nothing to show as a tangible return for the travel expenses. Some of the travel costs are even hidden to the company's accounting and considered private costs by the journalists, who feel personally involved in *Rue89* and its economic success. Along these same lines, Anastase, a former *Rue89* journalist, told me:

> The economic constraints are very internalized by the journalists. They always ask themselves how much it costs before doing anything. Even the photographeri— n order to borrow certain things for the cover of the magazine, which would cost 200

EUR. This is not good, because we cannot only think about this. Otherwise we don't do anything. (Interview with Anastase, March 2011)

For Anastase, the permanent attempt to reduce costs implied sacrifices that were not journalistically justifiable; the risk is that no journalistic activity is undertaken and the public is not informed.

In this chapter, I have chosen three critical moments, exemplifying three ways in which pragmatic compromises were contested when editorial and management principles clashed. Then, new negotiations started and new composite situations were arranged to realize yet another compromise. These three critical moments were: (1) the development of the printed magazine, (2) the last round of raising capital by attracting shareholders, and (3) the acqi sition of *Rue89* by *Le Nouvel Observateur* in December 2011.

GROWTH STRATEGY AND THE DEVELOPMENT OF THE PRINTED MAGAZINE

After establishing its "core" as the information revolution promised on the website, *Rue89* started expanding its operations. As the founders told us, they soon realized that they needed to diversify their areas of operation in order to increase revenue, to decrease their dependence on advertising income, and to continue innovating. Just a few months after the launch of the website, they started offering web design services; later they engaged themselves in new media training activities.

In the spring of 2011, Jules, a founder, explained several times that many of *Rue89*'s development initiatives were born and run without money: "A lot of things can be done without money." It seemed to me that they believed that moneyless interpersonal and interorganizational relations would drive development and lead to revenues. Jules acqi red this wisdom over years as an entrepreneur and told me many stories about development initiatives, new projects, or other changes at *Rue89*, which happened by chance and did not involve any contractual framing. One example concerned an event that happened a couple of days before the launch of the website, when a manager of a small company contacted *Rue89* to offer a real office for some months at no cost. If this had been the first time *Rue89* received a free, concrete offer to help its development, it was certainly not the last. One day a technology expert and passionate reader of *Rue89* offered them a complimentary iPhone app he had developed.

Yet another example of a moneyless development at *Rue89* was the local versions of the website. *Rue89* readers were concentrated mainly in Paris and the surrounding Île de France, but as soon as the brand received media attention and became well known, the founders received offers to make local versions in other French cities. About a year after the launch, there was even an attempt to launch *Rue89 Montréal*, which is inactive today.

The stories told to me about these events revealed pride in the staff's ability to sustain the development of *Rue89* in many directions with little or no financial investment. And the potential of increased revenue made many of these projects appealing to the entrepreneurs, who longed to break even. The website was dependent upon the opportunity to receive benevolent proposals from sympathizers who would support and contribute to its development not necessarily because they expected a financial return, but because they supported the ideals of the *Rue89*. In fact, they often explained their generosity by citing their ideological similarity to those ideals. Such a serendipitous development, as it was called at *Rue89*, did not happen without friction. Some initiatives, first seen as potentially good ways of developing the website and make more money for a low investment, created organizational tensions in their development.

One of these projects was the monthly printed magazine, *Revue89*. It was launched on 16 June 2010 and published for nearly two years. It was born with the idea of giving online papers a longer life and possibly a new readership. Announced as "the little sister" of *Rue89*, *Revue89* was presented as a magazine that would provide the opportunity for the most loyal readers and new readers to find "the best of *Rue89* in another format, with a selection of the most relevant comments, and an original 'mise-en-scène'" (Haski, 2010).

The print publication, I later understood, was not simply a paper version of the website; it introduced some critical changes in the organization of the newswork at *Rue89*. I focus here on two aspects that seemed particularly significant in reframing the organizational compromise between journalism and management at *Rue89*: (1) work for the website and work for the magazine now reqi red coordination, and (2) articles needed to be judged worthy of the magazine in order to be published.

Coordinating Work between *Rue89* and *Revue89*

I could easily see a difference in the tempo and atmosphere of work, especially when passing the door of the big newsroom to the training room, where the small team of magazine workers was located. This room was much calmer than the adjacent website newsroom and was divided into sections. There was an area used for training programs, with a projector and U-shaped desks. There was an area with a small library with the champagne fridge and a red sofa on which I conducted many interviews. And there was an area closer to the entrance where the magazine team worked. The magazine was produced by a small editorial team comprising part-time employees, including a magazine editor, a graphic designer, a photographer, and a proofreader. The selection of articles to be published in the magazine was made by the magazine editor, in collaboration with one of the chief editors, as determined by monthly rotation.

The monthly working cycle consisted of two parts. In the first two weeks of the month, the magazine team members worked mainly on other assignments and did not sit together at *Rue89*. The magazine editor checked the website continuously, searching for articles that could be published in the magazine, and the website editors were also assigning possible magazine subjects to the journalists. In the last two weeks of the month, the work for the magazine became more intense, and I would often see the magazine team gathered in their room at *Rue89* working long hours almost silently next to each other. In their space, the magazine editor or the graphic designer attached the progressively designed pages of the magazine to the wall, following a continuously updated scheme called *chemin de fer* (flat plan). It reminded me of a traditional magazine newsroom, yet it was different.

As many researchers and practitioners have noticed, online and print publications have different workflow rhythms, which was one of the main challenges of organizing integrated online̶of fline newsrooms (Raviola, 2010). It was usually newspaper companies that attempted to organize the co-existence— separated or integrated̶of the traditional print news production with the new online news. The situation at *Rue89* was reversed: The existing online news production was to expand into print. Still, the issue of different tempos remained, as noted by one of the magazine team members:

> We follow our own rhythm. As keen as I was on our being integrated in the Newsroom [the first two issues of the magazine were produced in an office outside *Rue89* location], we are still not integrated in the everyday sense of the everyday turmoil. We have a selection to make from the website; we have to choose what to make permanent. Anything that animates the website day by day̶ he hot news, *the* HuffPos [the *Huffington Post* look-alike], doesn't interest us. We look for subjects that are often narrower, as it's more difficult for us to present big, important subjects. ()..
> So, are we completely in the newsroom or a little bit on the side? We take advantage of the traction of the newsroom, which is a real machine in permanent movement. Yet we cannot be in permanent movement, because we need some distance. We make a magazine and we need to make a product that is going to last one month, and from that point of view this is very different from the culture of *Rue89*. (Interview with Robin, April 2011)

The co-existence of the two teams was not a trivial issue. Were they separate or integrated? What was to be their relationship with each other? As the magazine was dependent on the content produced and published on the website, some coordination was needed, and it happened in many ways. The chief editorial team of the website was involved in editing the magazine, for example. One member of that team̶ omprising the founders and the vice-editor-in-chief—

took turns each month helping the magazine team, especially for qe stions involving the cover and possible articles to publish. The chief editors also shared new ideas for magazine content with the magazine editor. The magazine editor also engaged in discussions with the website journalists when editing their articles to make them fit for printing, and sometimes contacted authors of articles outside the newsroom to obtain agreement on publishing their work in the magazine.

The coordination of work between *Rue89* and *Revue89* went smoothly most of the time, but sometimes it raised tension. It became clear to many journalists in the newsroom that business would not continue as usual after the launch of the magazine. The publishability of certain articles was considered in the weekly and monthly planning of newswork; longer reportages on specific themes were planned, bearing in mind that the magazine was a publication outlet. Not everyone was pleased with this new task. As Gervaise said in an interview, the magazine "messed up" the workflow:

> At the beginning, it should have been just a "best of" [a collection of the best articles], where we would not need to do anything. ().. In the end, we had to do a lot of things ourselves. Which means that when [the time comes to print the magazine], the editors are not there in the newsroom, as they follow the magazine publication closely. Many of the journalists work on it too, so it is a mess in the newsroom. We are understaffed and stressed out. (Interview with Gervaise, June 2011)

Coordinating the website and the magazine work became a specific task not only for the chief editors, but also for the journalists whose articles were going to be published in the magazine, thus straining the daily workflow in the website newsroom. In simple words, everybody realized that publishing a magazine took time, and that time devoted to the magazine competed with time spent on the website. Conseqe ntly, a qe stion was raised: Did the magazine make it worth stealing time from the website?

The planning of certain reportages for the magazine sometimes changed the rhythm of the work in the newsroom, because it introduced deadlines that would not exist otherwise. For cold, long-term reportages that are not sensitive to a publication date, the magazine deadline also represented the website deadline. *Rue89* had a rule that the website had to be published first or that the two had to be published simultaneously. This rule could interfere with the urgency and priority of news for the website and "force journalists to make things qi cker than they would otherwise have done", as one journalist observed.

Although the magazine's publication was introduced with the idea of not interfering with the normal workflow of the website, in practice it introduced and routinized the activity of planning longer reportages. As *Rue89* was a participatory website, coordination was needed not only between the magazine team and the *Rue89* journalists, but also with others involved in the *Rue89* news cycle—ike bloggers or readers, whose texts were considered for publication in the magazine. This coordination could raise some tension between the *Rue89* organization and the other non-journalist contributors to the website. Several journalists referred to the example of a blogger who saw texts published in print, became upset, and decided to leave *Rue89*, describing the reasons in a blogpost:

> I took my disappointment with patience. I knew that it was for a good reason and I loved you (I think I still love you). Yes, except that with your new conqe st, the magazine, I could not stand it any longer. Because the magazine, it's a military regime, there is no way to discuss any longer.
> I threatened you about my departure for the first time after the first magazine issue, and you told me that you would apologize. That it was the beginning; you admitted that you had done wrong, and you promised me that it would be better next time. Then you forgot to do all this. You started to forget a lot of things. I forgave you each time, because when there is love... but each time I was sadder and sadder. And you did not see anything.

The blogger compared blogging on the website to a love story with *Rue89* and described the way in which the love story got worse and worse. The publication of articles in magazine form were considered unacceptable, because it was perceived as a betrayal of the spirit of *Rue89* as a fluid and always-in-transformation participatory website. Nothing can be changed once it is in print, and there is no participation. The blogger lamented that this set the website in another type of relationship with non-journalist contributors. This criticism of was not the only negative message that *Rue89* received from readers and bloggers. But then the criticism started growing among the journalists.

Evaluating Work between *Rue89* and *Revue89*

Revue89 was born with the idea of giving online articles a longer life. As the number of pages was limited, it was necessary to be selective about the articles that would be printed and to edit them to suit the format of the magazine. Time became an issue in deciding which articles to include in the monthly magazine; only articles judged to be of long-lasting interest were to be published in print. The magazine team browsed the website every day to search for texts that would maintain their relevance over time. As they considered most of what was written for the web not to be publishable in print, it was a time-consuming task.

Although the monthly magazine introduces a judgment of monthly durability of news, magazine sales are concentrated in the week following publication. As Céleste explained to me, "They assess the news publishable on the magazine in order to exclude the hottest pieces, but at the same time, for the readers, the magazine seems to be a weekly rather than a monthly read" (Interview with Céleste, June 2011).

Time was a key element in the evaluation of work for the website as well. It was clear to everybody in the organization that speed and freqe nt updates were important. The goal is to attract readers to visit the website regularly and thus increase the number of pageviews, which is good for advertising. It was a common wisdom in the newsroom that longer reportage and slower publication pace would mean fewer clicks. Against this background, the magazine introduced another way of conceptualizing time: The longevity of articles was important to make the magazine saleable and valuable for the month. The two senses of time did not necessarily need to be in conflict, but the publication of the magazine certainly made the judgment of journalistic work at *Rue89* more complex.

There was no unanimous agreement about this development in the newsroom, because some of the journalists considered the magazine a sign of appreciation for their work. As Kim, an intern, put it:

> ... what I find very funny, and perhaps I am wrong, but I have the impression that being published in the magazine is really a bit of a,... not a promotion, but an appreciation. The journalists appreciate being published in the magazine. It is very funny for a pure player! (Interview with Kim, June 2011)

With this hint in mind, I asked other journalists about it. Maxime replied: "Actually, if you never have an article in the magazine, it means that you don't write well enough for it to be passed there" (Interview with Maxime, June 2011).

The journalists varied over time in their reasons for including or excluding an article from *Revue89*. Some of the journalists reflected on the fact that at the beginning they interpreted the publication of their article in the magazine only as a *quality judgment*. Later they realized that there are many other reasons for deciding if an article is publishable in the magazine.

> Yes, it is often articles that have received a lot of clicks, but it is not an indicator of qa lity. One of our best journalists on this website has written perhaps one of [that person's] worst articles by reporting on [name of a public person], and it has been published in the magazine because they needed a subject with a lot of pictures. I did a little thing on prostitutes ().. and it was selected for the magazine. But I've done things really more important that haven't been published. So, it [number of clicks] doesn't mean anything.

Several others told me that they had reflected upon it, but they concluded that whether they were published in the magazine or not was irrelevant. They concluded that publication in the magazine depended on the type of article

rather than the qa lity of the journalistic work. Some of the journalists, especially those who had been at *Rue89* for a long time, refused to think about the
re-publication of their articles in the magazine. In their eyes, the website was
the core of *Rue89*, and it was its readers they had in mind when writing. This
disenchantment with the magazine evolved over time as they watched with
perplexity the choices made for the print publication:

> It isn't a value judgment. I think it is good, but it is frustrating, because we do
> super investigations on *Rue89*, which are not republished in the magazine. To me,
> they are more representative of *Rue89* than certain things that are in the magazine.
> I wouldn't know exactly how they choose. They make their own choices. (Interview
> with Maxime, June 2011)

Some journalists were concerned about the contradictions introduced by the
magazine, viewing them as inconsistent with the core idea of participation and
as introducing tension into the organization of work.

In the spring of 2012, after almost two years of publication, the magazine
was finally closed down. There were two reasons given: (1) because sales were
not contributing enough to the company's profitability, and (2) because an
iPad application was judged to be more in line with the innovative character of
Rue89. Some members of the magazine team were transformed into the iPad
team, and some left the company.

INCREASING CAPITAL

Achieving breakeven remained an unreached goal for *Rue89*, despite its
numerous development projects and the founders' economic attitude, which
consisted of saving as much money as possible and avoiding risks. *Rue89*
came close to breakeven, but costs continued to be higher than revenues.
Conseqe ntly, the founders resorted to raising capital by attracting new shareholders, thereby covering losses and providing cash for the upcoming period.

The term *levé de fonds* (fundraising) was often used at *Rue89* to describe
the process of attracting capital from various investors, whether individuals or
companies, that would acqi re shares in *Rue89*. Thus the percentage of founders' shares diminished over time. In the beginning, the shareholding capital
of the company was approximately 100,000 EURe– ash that the founders
had invested and had used to attract and pay staff. When cash became scarce
because of low income and because the founders' initial investment had been
used, it was time to generate increased capital, which can usually be acqi red
through loans or shareholding capital. In the case of *Rue89*, however, the
founders told me that it was difficult to borrow money from banks, so they had
to finance their growth by acqi ring new shareholders.

In this chapter, I focus on one specific round of capital increase that happened during my time of observation in the organization. A key feature of this capital increase is its development into a critical moment for the main organizational compromise of *Rue89*, holding together editorial principles and economic constraints. It is precisely the development of this critiqe that I want to analyze here.

When we met *Rue89*'s editors and journalists for the first time in December 2010, they all anticipated that they would achieve breakeven during the following year— hat they were already close. In early spring of 2011, however, they realized that breakeven was further away than they had believed and decided to raise capital by attracting new shareholders to cover their losses and to invest in the development of the organization. This was the fourth capital increase in the history of *Rue89*.

Announcing New Money Internally

During the spring, the founders called for a strategy meeting in the meeting and training room during lunch time. It lasted for 90 minutes, and every member of the organization was invited. The founders started the meeting by presenting the results for 2010. Visitors and visits had increased by 45%, especially in the fourth qa rter. Total revenues were 1.6 million EUR, of which 68% were advertising revenues; 29% were training and consulting revenues; and 3.5% constituted other revenue sources, like sales of merchandise. Costs had also increased, but less than revenues had. Some of the new projects, like the magazine, had contributed positively to the company's finances: The magazine generated profits of 38,000 EUR in 2010. As a result, losses had diminished by 45%.

After this review, they moved to discuss the reorganization of the newsroom. As a few journalists had left and newcomers had joined the newsroom, there had been a few adjustments in the distribution of subjects among the remaining journalists. New recruitsone   reporter and one or two desk editorsw- ere also announced. This issue triggered some initial qe stions in the room, as the types and numbers of recruits were often discussed by journalists in the newsroom. The discussion was kept short at this point, however, as the founders wanted to move on and give the big news. As Jules explained:

> There were two possible choices. One was to obtain the breakeven point by tightening the belt. The other was to raise funds and create new projects, such as tablets, sports, or other things, and to improve the working and living conditions of the company. We decided to do that. (Fieldnotes, April 2011)

Now the news had been revealed. Gabriel continued, specifying that they would choose projects that would be sure or nearly sure to be profitable. Up to this point, the meeting had been running qi te smoothly without open discussion. After this point, however, the discussion became increasingly heated, and the validity of the current organizational compromise was challenged.

Although the founders tried to justify themselves by saying that a fundraising project was underway to improve salaries and working conditions— hat they weren't merely using cost cutting to achieve breakeven—many critical voices were raised, and an intense debate developed. Voices succeeded one another qi ckly, and I remember the physical sensation of being present at that meeting. As the tone of the discussion became more heated, my feeling of discomfort increased, and I tended not to look into anyone's eyes, as if my presence would pass unnoticed if my eyes did not connect with theirs.

Critical qe stioning developed along two main lines: (1) the appropriateness of the way journalistic work was organized, and (2) the ability to sustain the qa lity of the website.

The organizational critiqe featured the qe stion of what was going to be done, concretely, to improve working conditions and how it was going to be done. Two questions were particularly dear to the hearts of the employed journalists: salary increases and new recruitments. The two issues were intertwined in a flow of challenges to what was emerging as the management team:

> Yannick: Will the salaries be increased? Because we work really hard for what we're paid!
> Jules: It's included in [what I've called] improvement of the working conditions of the company.

Gabriel confirmed, but specified that it would be donenot now, but after the fundraising.

> Céleste: In six months then? [This would mean after the summer.]
> Gabriel: No, before the summer.
> Sam: And when are we going to have the economics journalist?
> Gabriel: After the fundraising.
> Marley: We have the impression of having already heard this story eight months ago.

To support the organizational critiqe , some journalists brought up the number of people leaving *Rue89* as proof of the inappropriateness of the current organizational compromise and the necessity of changing it. At *Libération*, a journalist reported, they wonder if they should write a piece about *Rue89*, as there have been 8 departures in 13 months. In their defense, one of the editors responded that they were also thinking of writing and publishing an article on

Libé, a news company that does not manage to pay its employees. With this response, the editor dismissed the journalist's challenge by referring to the common difficulties for news organizations to make money and sustain themselves economically. Journalists stressed that people leaving *Rue89* presented a problemnot only because good colleagues left the organization, but also because the organization of work suffered from turnover and lack of recruitment to replace departing colleagues.

The critiqe of the organizational compromise moved to include a critiqe of the basic economic model that was conceived to support journalism at *Rue89*. Toward the end of the meeting, in fact, Gervaise, who had been relatively qi et until then, jumped into the conversation and spoke out "as a shareholder", complaining that the leadership of the organization underestimated the importance of the newsroom: "So, instead of distributing a thousand bricks around the project, it would be better to pile the bricks vertically on one project and make the newsroom really stronger." This line of reasoning was challenging perceptions of what was considered worthy of investment for the success of *Rue89*: Should they differentiate the sources of income, or should they invest everything in the newsroom and make journalism the only source of revenue?

The discussion became even more intense when the issue shifted to conseqe nces of decreased website quality on the newsroom organization. Some of the reporters said that the website was losing the uniqe ness of the initial innovation and that there were lower-qa lity articles being placed in the central column of the websitet— he position that should feature the most relevant and highest quality articles, There were too many projects, they argued, and they were moving toward more general coverage and abandoning more pointed and sharper articles on a limited number of subjects.

One of the founders, Dominiqe , disagreed with this critiqe : "This week was very good." Loan, a journalist, confirmed Dominiqe 's point of view, saying that the website had improved consistently and that the new journalists contributed a great deal. The discussion continued, however:

> Dominiqe : All the letters of the PORSCHE are in balance, but there is a weak R for reactivity. [PORSCHE is an acronym for Participatory, Open, Reactive, Serendipitous, Collective, Humorous, and Enqi ringt— he watchwords of *Rue89*]
>
> Yannick: We don't have discussions on journalism any longer. We talk a lot about the organization and the money, but we talk very little about how to treat the different subjects, which angle to tackle them from. When Max [a former *Rue89* journalist] was here, the purpose of the morning conference was to say: "Do we have an angle? No? Then we don't do it." Now we're more likely to hear, "Here's a subject. We do it. You're going to do it."
>
> Jackie (editor): Sometimes I do read some papers and pass them on to the desk editors and if they don't think they're good, they don't get published.

Repeating critical discussions that I heard several times at *Rue89*, some lamented that *Rue89* had lost its innovativeness, as at that point every newspaper in the nation had started engaging its readership by opening a comments section to the public. Just a few weeks before this meeting, on 11 March 2011, a powerful earthqa ke and tsunami had hit Northeastern Japan, instigating a major nuclear accident in Fukushima. Most of the established news organizations had used microblogging[4] to cover the event live, had opened up the possibility for readers to comment on the articles, and had appealed to readers with connections to Japan to help in reporting on the news. It became evident then that what was once an innovative feature of *Rue89* had been embraced by all the established newspapers.

The journalists that spoke most openly and engaged themselves in the discussions were *les historiques* (the historical ones)t— hose who had been in the organization the longest. The founders responded by declaring themselves well aware of the salary problem, which they said they had proven by their own example. They also had decreased their own salaries significantly, they said. One of *les historiques* reported a salary that was one-third of that received at a former newspaper. A journalist gave a summarized perception of the main message from the meeting a few weeks later: "We're in deep shit, but we're all there. We all want our company to work. We love our company".. (Fieldnotes, April 2011).

The heated discussion ended with an agreement to hold a lunch meeting the first Friday of each month to discuss internal issues, especially of a journalistic nature. One critical moment was therefore resolved by planning for other critical moments, and the time in between was filled by a lower-tempo and lower-intensity everyday critiqe . This resolution was typical of *Rue89*, where everyday work could so easily end up in more substantial discussions about the future of journalism and often in self-critiques about the level of innovativeness and the qa lity of journalism. This direction was not unlike the direction of conversations in a laboratory where scientists engage in epistemological discussions around the significance of their instruments and the validity of science. In fact, the staff often talked about *Rue89* as a lab.

Elaborating on What to do With the New Money

Everybody returned to work after the strategy meeting broke up after 90 minutes, but tensions were still in the air. The days, weeks, and months after

---

[4] . Microblogging is used often in breaking news coverage and it refers to the use of technical solutions allowing very short and freqe nt updates or comments on a given news or themes.

this heated meeting, there were still traces of the discussions that had broken out, albeit in a less heated form; many everyday conversations continued to develop the debate that had been opened that day. The experience seems to have been different for different groups of employees, but it seems to have marked a key moment in the organizational life of *Rue89*. Old-timers recognized a rehearsed internal debate about the path to independence and the appropriateness of strategic and organizational choices for the success of *Rue89*. To the newer recruits, who had been more silent at the meeting, and some of whom had told me in interviews that they were relatively uninterested in the financial side of the organization, the meeting represented a crucial revelation: They realized how much *Rue89* was not only a journalistic newsroom, but also a company, and how much the financial aspect was a significant issue of debate. The leading team recognized that they had been taken aback by the strong reactions of the journalists. They thought they were bringing a piece of good news to the newsroom, but they were widely criticized.

After the meeting, most of the journalists agreed on the appropriateness of the decision to raise capital in order to bring more money into the organization, and they saw this move as a sign of development. There were disagreements, however, around what this development should look like and how the upcoming money should be used.

Many of the journalists deemed it appropriate to raise capital as a way of financing journalistic development, in light of the upcoming presidential election in 2012. Stéphane, for example, stressed the importance of having money to spend when the campaign started:

> I prefer to know that we'll grow next year, rather than trying to make savings everywhere, which would worry me in the year of a presidential election. I don't want to save everywhere, not to be able to buy anythingI.. think it's good, as the presidential campaign starts in September, that we gather a lot of money and then we'll see. (Interview with Stéphane, June 2011)

Several journalists stressed the importance of increasing salaries as a valuable way of holding the organization together. As Alix, a young journalist, said:

> The raising of capital gives us a bigger margin of actions in order to pay better and avoid departures like that of [a journalist], which was also linked to the financial issue, but not only that ().. There was tension in the meeting, as the bosses were shocked to hear that the financial issue was one of the reasons for the departure. I think a "before and after the departure" attitude was created. Increasing the salaries is important because many journalists receive better offers from outside. (Fieldnotes, conversation with Alix, May 2011)

Several journalists complained of unfairness in the way salaries were set, noting discrepancies between salary levels and years working with the company. This issue seemed to be particularly urgent for the old-timer journalists, as they had been living on low salaries for a longer time and were waiting for the new capital to be used to give them some financial reward. Better salaries were considered crucial by the journalists not only because they needed to make a living, but as a recognition of their work and engagement in the company.

Another priority that many journalists considered worthy of investment was recruitment of new journalists. Too few journalists and too low salaries created a stressful working environment, according to the journalists, and were among the causes of some people leaving the company"— 11 people within 18 months", as Sam told me. More people and better salaries were what many journalists longed fora— ctions that would give them more time to focus on what they considered their core task: producing news for the website.

> Now I long even more for the team to be able to have some relief, because others continue to compare us to the big Internet media, like *lemonde.fr* and *lefigaro.fr*, but we have one-tenth the personnel. Obviously, we have a participatory model, which means that we have papers coming from outside, contributions of high qa lity, which come from researchers [for example]. But I would like to increase the editorial staff. (Fieldnotes, conversation with Maxime, May 2011)

Changes among the people working at *Rue89* also meant changes on the website and in the spirit of the organization, as many employees recognized. As Dominiqe used to say, "*Rue89* was changing its skin, like a snake", as new generations of employees were recruited. This transformation implied, among other things, a different engagement of the new journalists in the *Rue89* enterprise. In the beginning, volunteering journalists were given shares when they joined *Rue89*, but the newcomers did not own shares. The new journalists had joined *Rue89* more because of its journalistic reputation than to experiment with its possible financial models. They had experienced the heat of the debates following the capital increase with some detachment and saw the spring meeting as the last act of a period of departures which had changed *Rue89* into a normal company. As Sam observed:

> ... a little bit of life or death, which seemed to exist at the beginning. In any case, it is in this way that they tell the story with other words, but it comes back to this: "We are a little team. We are together. We have been through difficulties together. We will grow together." This story has changed. (Interview with Sam, June 2011)

Although in transformation in the spring of 2011, *Rue89* still carried signs of its initial organizational compromise between journalism and management, whereby profitability was believed to be fundamental to reaching editorial independence. It became clear in the process of critiqi ng that developed after the announcement of the capital increase that money was not simply a material tool to finance journalism; it was also used as a symbolic device for judging worth.

Money was a symbol of what was really considered important in the organization and, as such, its use was qe stioned. Once I met ex-employee Gervaise for coffee in a café, and the conversation turned to the strategy meeting and how irritated Gervaise had become:

> In fact, there was something that had disturbed me, but that I knew very, very well... There were two things in fact. On the one hand, they announced the budget numbers for 2010 with an increase of the personnel costs by 60% without one single euro for the journalists' salaries. Although I'd been advocating for a long time to be able to raise salaries for the reporters, I'm very well aware of the fact that it's an enterprise, but the basis of this enterprise remains the newsroom, and I find the investment decisions of *Rue89* to be really poor. (Interview with Gervaise, June 2011)

This young journalist had been with *Rue89* for a long time. Through this critiqe , Gervaise was articulating qe stions about the appropriateness of the founders' investment decisions, not only because of the belief that they hindered good journalism, but also because of *Rue89*'s poor financial reasoning. Gervaise accepted the organizational compromise between different frames of worth—journalism vs. management—but criticized the way in which this compromise was being practiced and sustained. To substantiate this critiqe , Gervaise mentioned all the people who had left the organization: The departure of "all the intermediary rings in generational terms" from the newsroom was a sign that the organizational compromise as it was practiced did not hold and needed to be changed. One of the sources of the problem was the fact that the founders were engaged in *Rue89* as journalists, managers, and owners. Although recognized by many as one of the strengths of the company, these multiple roles created some difficulties in practice, "sometimes in terms of time, sometimes in terms of decision-making" (Interview with Anastase, May 2011):

> When are you wearing the journalist hat? When are you wearing the boss of the enterprise hat? They have a lot of difficulty in separating the two. Do they want to do that? I don't think so. Jules recognized several times during the meetings of the "board of surveillance" that he had too often taken the hat of the boss of the enterprise. I was happy that he had recognized it, but we couldn't see any changes. (Interview with Anastase, May 2011)

Money was also a symbol of the worth that others assigned to the work performed at *Rue89*. The raising of capital was welcome not only because it made new money available for *Rue89*'s operations, but also because it was a sign that the company was considered valuable, both editorially and financially, by people outside the company. As Marley explained to me:

> The capital increase, which is taking place now, is going very well. The shareholders want to invest in *Rue89*, which is very good for us, because it shows that we always have very good editorial success, because it is the editorial which is at the heart of our profession. It shows also that these shareholders believe in our financial model, which is also a good thing, because at the moment we are not yet profitable. (Fieldnotes, conversation with Marley, May 2011)

Accepting the New Money and Making it Public

Over the months following the strategy meeting, internal discussions around the use of the new financial capital were trending down, and the founders were continuing to work toward obtaining as much capital as possible for the development of the company, all the while continuing to keep a majority of the shares. This capital increase was conducted with the consent and help of the larger shareholders, who were being kept informed through regular meetings with the founders. There was also a group of minor shareholders—*The Inhabitants of Rue89* who owned about 5% of *Rue89*'s capital and also needed to be informed.

The Inhabitants was the company created by *Rue89* for the journalists and technicians who had volunteered during the first three or four months of the *Rue89* project and who had been compensated with a few shares. Because these shareholders had automatically become shareholders in *Rue89*, they now owned capital in *Rue89*. Although they had all been company employees originally, with new recruitments and departures, this was no longer the case. Some tension emerged between employees who were not shareholders and shareholders who were no longer employees. In order to mitigate the tension, one of the oldest journalists, who had slightly more of The Inhabitants'[5] shares, decided to give some of them to the later recruits.

In June 2011, the annual general meeting of The Inhabitants was planned—an occasion for the founders to announce the results of the fundraising campaign to the whole organization. The assembly was treated as an extended gathering of present and past organizational members. The boundaries between being an employee and a shareholder in The Inhabitants had gotten complicated over the years: Some former employees who had worked as volunteers

---

[5]   The Inhabitants was the name of the company created by *Rue89* for the volunteers who had initially worked for the website. Shares of The Inhabitants were owned by journalists and technicians and The Inhabitants, became shareholders in *Rue89*. Thus, journalists and technicians owning shares of The Inhabitants were indirectly owning capital in *Rue89*.

when *Rue89* first began and had left the company after a few years, were still shareholders in The Inhabitants and thus connected with *Rue89*. On the other hand, there were employees who had been recruited after the autumn of 2017 when the company started paying salaries, who were not shareholders in The Inhabitants, despite the fact that they were still working for *Rue89*. At that assembly, the external shareholders' capital generated some critical qe stions about ownership and development of the company. One of the critical issues about ownership was the liqi dity of The Inhabitants' shares, which differed from those of the *Rue89* shares. Was it possible to sell The Inhabitants' shares? Or was it only the shares of *Rue89* that were liqi d? Was the ownership structure, as settled at the beginning of *Rue89*, still an acceptable compromise, or had it become outdated over the years with the evolution of the organization? These qe stions, raised and discussed during the assembly, echoed other debates and touched upon the general issue of eqa lity of engagement in *Rue89* for different groups of people—employees and founders, shareholders and non-shareholders, old and new employeesa— nd how much that engagement was worth now and in the future.

Once the shareholding capital increase was realized and approved by the general assembly, a public announcement was made on the website. An article was published on the blog called *Le blog du making of*, to inform the public about the success of the raising of capital and other projects, under the title "A capital increase to develop *Rue89*". The text, authored by Pierre Haski, the president of *Rue89*, presented the capital increase as a way for the company to pursue its development and as a piece of good news. He then specified what the development comprises:

> The development of the website goes through the improvement of its human means, the editorial qa lity, and the technical means. On this last point, our commentators will be able to discover in a few weeks a new platform and a new website design, and in the autumn a new mobile platform, developed with the new HTML5 technology. (Haski, 2011)

After specifying the three directions of *Rue89*'s developmenthum an, technological, and editorialP– ierre framed this increased capital in relation to the wider web landscape, which was increasingly competitive and financially complex, and in relation to the higher purpose of *Rue89*t— o build "an independent and participatory media, totally anchored in the digital revolution" (Haski, 2011). As he wrote:

> But the growing position of the website in the media landscape must be accompanied by a financial model that avoids losing money, a condition of independence, and also finances the developments, both human and technical. This economic battle

on the web is complex, and the new means we have been provided have to allow us to win it. (Haski, 2011)

Echoing the participatory philosophy of *Rue89*, Pierre then called for the support of two groups outside the group of employees, to win the battle. He argued that it is *Rue89*'s higher purpose that the *shareholders* support and participate in the development of the organization, and it is only with the trust and participation of the *residents* (members of the website) that this purpose can be reached.

Readers posted a total of 119 comments to this announcement. As usual, some were critical and others were supportive. The positive commentators saw the capital increase as a way of developing the website and some of them wondered about the possibility of involving readers directly in the financing of the company. The commentator Gérard COVOS, for example, wondered:

> @Pierre Haski. And would it be inappropriate or too "dangerous" for your editorial policy to launch a national subscription through the residents?
> Or for the democratic exercise it would conceive?

Other readers, for example, Hannibal Forez, suggested a more radical alternative to the ownership structure of *Rue89*:

> On the capital: Why not allow the participation of the readers (like *Le Monde*)? I would be happy to buy some shares in *Rue89*.

The critical commentators debated whether an increase in the shareholders' base and a reliance on advertising as a source of income would guarantee independence or would it be an inevitable sign of dependence and failure of the chosen business model. Shaziza, for example, addressed the president of *Rue89*:

> []. . So Mr. HASKI, with all the respect I have for you, stop making us laugh with your story of the independence. Your website, like all the other news websites, is not profitable today. If the main shareholders leave tomorrow, the main shareholders leave, and *Rue89* will plunge.

For this reader and many others, the proof of independence would be that *Rue89* could sustain itself without external shareholders investing in the company and potentially influencing the direction of the newswork in one way or another. Profit is understood here as the means to independence, like the founders of *Rue89* had often argued. The loss of profit and the necessity of resorting to the pockets of shareholders were proofs of failed independence.

Others stressed that the reliance on state subsidies was to be taken into account when addressing independence. As the commentator *Rue des oeillasres* wrote:

> [t.. he condition of independence].. Oh yes? We don't have the same definition of independence... some news websites don't have the hundreds of thousands of euros of state subsidies (well, some don't have at all, they are then INDEPENDENT) and more freqe ntly visited than you, while proposing articles that are not coming out of the mediocre pen which your biased statements reveal at every single letter.

Other readers connected the discussion about *Rue89*'s independence to a wider critiqe of capitalism and expressed disappointment in *Rue89* as a project of resistance to capitalism and the utopia of the free web. A freqe nt commentator, Pierre, wrote:

> But it is a real scandal!
> I thought that *Rue89* wanted to distance itself from this capitalistic mechanism, which goes through shareholding.

I read this comment as carrying a good dose of irony, although it is interesting that wider ideological debates are mobilized here to discuss the appropriateness of the capital increase signed by *Rue89*. This type of comment was not usual in the community of *Rue89* residents, as the website was profiled as a left-leaning publication from the beginning: Many of the commentators, especially those engaged from the beginning of the website, believed that its ownership structure often challenged the independence of *Rue89*. Many of the commentators identified as Communists or radically left-leaning, and believed that *Rue89* should not be a corporation and should not have shareholderst— hat it should exist merely as a project pulling together the desires to realize an open participatory community for news production and to develop a successful journalistic enterprise. The commentators suggested that *Rue89* could take a different organizational forma— cooperative, for example, or another form of non-profit organization.

All these lines of critiqe , which were somewhat suspended after the capital increase and routinized in the everyday news machines of *Rue89*, surfaced again and in increased complexity in the next critical moment analyzed here: the acqi sition of *Rue89*.

THE ACQUISITION

Financial independence, so dear to the founders of *Rue89* as a guarantee of editorial independence, was an everyday struggle. Breakeven was a moving and missed target for entrepreneurs who tried to reconcile their journalistic ideals and management principles in the organizing of their daily work. Over the years, because of a shortage of cash, the founders of *Rue89* had rejected a number of solutions, which would certainly have gotten them closer to breakeven, but further away from their journalistic and organizational ideals. As Dominiqe explained to me:

> Discussions like this [how to increase cash] we had last year too. We have a problem: [We could] fire half the team. You know, this kind of attitude... Or, your traffic [the number of clicks] is weak: Why don't you do more celebrities, or track news... We want to remain master of our company and the way we operate... We're not creating a cash machine; we're not trying tow- e're not here to lower the standards of journalism we aspire to or lower the social conditions [of employed journalists]. We've tried to keep the standards. And we feel that it's hard with some investors [becoming shareholders]. Maybe we have a negative view of investors. (Interview with Dominiqe , December 2010)

It was critical for the founders to keep the majority of the ownership, as they did not want the other shareholders to influence the management of the company. They had a selective view of who could and should become shareholders in *Rue89*, and despite the several rounds of raising shareholding capital, the total shares of the founders remained the largest portion of shares; as of the last capital increase in June 2011, they owned a little over 40% of the company.

In the autumn of 2011, the management team of *Rue89*, the so-called *directoire*, drafted the budget for 2012 and realized that their economic situation was very tense. A few years later, one of them recalled a gloomy budget meeting:

> And in the autumn of 2011, I remember a dinner at [the name of a place]. We had a budget meeting and at the end of the meeting my wife, who had not been sitting at our table, told me: "Your meeting seemed to be a little bit tough. There were long periods of silence." And, actually, it was very difficult, because we had a budget... which we would have made it through if 100% of the objectives were reached. Which one can never do, if you ask me. If there had been a little accident, like an advertising contract that wouldn't go through or was canceled or an economic recession, we would have been in a really difficult position. So, we adopted this budget, which was unrealistic, because it never happens to meet 100% of one's own objectives. (Interview with a founder, January 2017)

Some weeks later, the general director of the weekly magazine, *Le Nouvel Observateur*,[6] who had also worked at *Libération*, contacted the founder. They had been in contact several times over the previous few months with the owner of *Le Nouvel Observateur*, as he had become a shareholder of the company

---

[6]   *Le Nouvel Observateur* was also called *Le Nouvel Obs*, *Nouvel Obs*, and *L'Obs* by both journalists and the general public. I use some of these nicknames in this chapter. In October 2014, the name was officially changed to *L'Obs*.

during the last round of acqi ring capital. During the previous year, he had tried to acqi re the company, but the founders rejected his offer in the name of independence. This time was different.

Negotiating and Publicly Announcing the Acquisition

This time *Le Nouvel Observateur* contacted the pure playerna me given to online-only news websitest— o make a new offer of acqi sition. The founder recalled how they continued the discussions they had at their budget meeting:

> We asked ourselves whether it isn't more reasonable today to protect oneself within a group, and if we had the choice in the Paris marketplace, with which group would we like to work? Perdriel [Claude Perdriel, the owner of *Le Nouvel Observateur*] had an advantage, which was that his was a family owned group, a personal group, left leaning, and owned by someone older, without ambitions of the stock exchange and so on. His wealth comes from his industrial activity and he uses his industry wealth to finance the media operations. (Interview with a founder, January 2017)

So, the founders were seduced by the owner of *Le Nouvel Observateur* and his story, as one of them admitted. This monthly magazine had a reputation of old-fashioned, quality journalism, and its owner, Claude Perdriel, 84 years old when he acqi red *Rue89*, was known as a "kind", left-leaning media patron, moved by his passion for literature and for journalists. He was often portrayed as "Father Christmas replenishing the losses of his newspapers with the money gained in the business of sanitary facilities" (Grosjean, 2014), such as toilets and other household fixtures and appliances. The founders of *Rue89* accepted the acqi sition of their website and company with the promise of being able to help the old and dusty *Le Nouvel Observateur* to renew itself. On 21 December 2011, an announcement was published on *Rue89*:

> Under the leadership of Claude Perdriel, *Le Nouvel Observateur* and *Rue89* have decided to come closer together, with the aim of reinforcing their editorial and economic independence in an environment in full transformation. (*Rue89*, 2011)

In this statement, both editorial and economic independence are mentioned as being reinforced by the two companies coming "closer together". The change of *Rue89*'s ownership was framed as being aimed at retaining financial and editorial independence. A new organizational compromise was advanced, shifting the original entrepreneurial journalism into an online news subsidiary in a larger media group. The announcement continued by explaining the relationship between the two companies in the new organizational compromise:

> This decision will be effective as of December 31st this year. It will allow two enterprises to benefit mutually from their expertise and from the uniqe position that

this act gives to their digital offer, with a complete proposition in all the segments of news.

The founders of *Rue89* and their team will continue to develop the activity of *Rue89* within Claude Perdriel's group to reinforce their position as "pure player".

A press conference will be organized at the beginning of the year to present the project.

This decision underlines the importance of the digital strategy within the group *Le Nouvel Observateur* and expresses the confidence that it places in the development of its activities on the Internet. (*Rue89*, 2011)

This announcement emphasized the expertise of *Rue89* in making digital journalism and the potential influence that this expertise would be given within a wider *Le Nouvel Observateur* group. In a way, the agreement between the founders of *Rue89* and Claude Perdriel implied the exchange of capital for digital news expertise: A market transaction, in which *Rue89* was sold to a buyer who agreed to lead to a new organizational compromise that would help hold together editorial and management principles in ways that the previous arrangements had failed to do. In the statements of two owners:

> Claude Perdriel: "I have felt the greatest professional respect for *Rue89* since its creation. I am very happy with this good relationship with the founders, which will allow us to better adapt to the fast evolution of the web."
>
> Pierre Haski: "The founders of *Rue89* are happy about this agreement with Claude Perdriel and the *Le Nouvel Observateur* Group, which allows [us] to make the *Rue89* adventure permanent, all by guaranteeing its editorial independence. Together, we will be able to better pick up the exciting challenges of the digital revolution and guarantee qa lity news." (*Rue89*, 2011)

Negotiations about the acqi sition had been ongoing since November 2011. Because a clause in the negotiations reqi red secrecy, the founders could not talk about it until an agreement was reached. On 21 December 2011, they heard rumors of leaks about the acqi sition negotiations, and they decided to go public with it. The same day, they announced the decision to the rest of the organization and to the public. This was shocking for manype ers, employees, and readersa— nd raised strong feelings and critiqe s from many sides.

One of the main points of critiq e was the loss of independence. The founders tried to frame the acqi sition as a way of making *Rue89* permanent as an economic enterprise and guaranteeing "editorial independence". On the day of the announcement, an article was published on the website, originally entitled "Alliance between *Rue89* and *Le Nouvel Observateur*" and then "*Rue89* joins *Le Nouvel Observateur* Group", where the relationship was framed as an "alliance", and it was explained that the "agreement is materialized by the acqi sition of *Rue89* capital by Claude Perdriel".

The founders of *Rue89* stressed the importance of maintaining their independence, which they now denoted mainly with the adjective "editorial". As reported in many other newspapers and news media reports, the president of *Rue89* recognized that it was "partly a loss", but that the aim of this loss was to guarantee the survival and duration of the adventure that was *Rue89*. The founders continue to argue that *Rue89* remained a pure player and that it was business as usual.

This line of arguments— uggesting a new organizational compromise and presenting it as being as worthy of consideration as the previous onew— as not easy to defend with critiqe s coming from every side. Daniel Schneiderman, a renown former TV journalist and founder of the pure player *Arrêt sur Images*, wrote in an article published on his website the day after the announcement:

> Sadness. First of all, sadness in learning suddenly that our cousins from *Rue89* have just let themselves be bought by Claude Perdriel. Since 2007, we pulled hard at the oars side by side in our adventure as "pure players", as we say. Each one in his or her boat of course, but with some footbridge, being concerned about the other's health, being sincerely happy for the others' achievements and successes. It is over. At the dead-end, *Rue89* has chosen the boulevard. And it is sad. ()..
>
> A medium is a whole. Shareholding structure, financing sources, and content are not but one whole. A medium, even before it writes or says anything, is an address, a promise. The press of the Resistance [during World War II], Sartre's Libération, the free radios, all these media born of a fight and carried by a generation, were first of all promises. The wave of the pure players of 2007 is the most recent one. *Rue89*, like *Mediapart*, like us, like others everyday more numerous, have carried and carry the promise of a press that is liberated from the technical constraints of the old supports (it will continue), but also liberated from the old connivances with ()..
> what we call the establishment. In all these aspects, alas, I cannot see who could be more representative of the old media than *Le Nouvel Observateur*, with its cultural pages of deference, its arthritic pages of the typically French political politics, its timorous ideological and economic conformism, its falling-in-love stories of the winning capitalists, and its pages full of advertisements for watches showing that we have not missed our life (even if, careful, don't make me say what I have not said, there are also good articles in *Le Nouvel Observateur*). (Schneidermann, 2011)

Rue89 readers left many comments on the announcement of the acqi sition; 676 comments were posted on two articles announcing and discussing the acqi sition on the day of the press release. To all these comments, only one response from one of the founders was posted. The overwhelming consensus emerging from the comments was a critiqe over *Rue89*'s loss of independence and qe stioning of the effects of the new ownership on the editorial line of the website. Following is a sampling of the responses. As one of the commentators, *hanslebvre*, wrote:

> As the capital has been acqi red 100%, how to be sure to keep one's independence and one's own editorial line? Well, let's not jeopardize the future...
> With regard to the ɋa lity of *nouvel obs* [nickname for *Le Nouvel Observateur*], let me contest it vividly! Well, it is a [publishing] house that has become ɋi te dull, where the vacuity often leads to focus on celebrities.
> ().. I cannot but wish that *Rue89* keeps its little exotic approach to news.

Another commentator, youla, said:

> What a delusion. [The game is] over; as for independence, we already felt a while ago that the editorial line was becoming more and more mainstream.
> Now, it is done, I am really not optimistic for what follows.
> *Rue89* will soon (already?) be synonymous with the dominant thinking.
> Hoping that you will keep at least the freedom of expression intact in the comments.
> Sad news.

Youla was followed by the commentator communeux:

> So, independence failed, as actually it is the *nouvel obs* that bought the capital.
> As for transparency, where is it? Clearly, how much has the capital sale brought and to whom?
> A response at the level of your independence is awaited...

Stasles added:

> One that sells toilets buys *Rue89*? The logic is respected, as a sport journalist would say.
> Otherwise, congrats for the new language: Being financially dependent is being independent.

And Philippe Blasco wrote:

> What is the strength of *Rue89*; it is, to my understanding, neither its founders nor its journalists, not its editorial line, as we find the same thing a little bit everywhere on the other media; its strength is its community of users, which has even given itself a name: the neighbors.
> It is annoying and risky to join a media group which is largely established and thus an integral part of the media system.
> The neighbors will be attentive to the smallest change with an obviously suspicious eye.
> And as *Rue89* is nothing without its neighbors, then it is annoying and amazingly risky.
> The future will be interesting, and I am looking forward to seeing what follows!

One of the founders, adding a comment to respond to the readers, wrote:

> The neighbors and their comments are an important part of the originality, of the identity, of the mission, and of the success of *Rue89*. But it is not all. Not to mention but two other aspects: our ability to put forward voices in society that we hear only a little, or yet the capacity of our team to give an original tone, to choose displaced subjects, to inform you in a different way than when you open the tap of the luke-warm information continuously supplied.

It was not only peers and readers who reacted critically to the acqi sition; it was also the journalists, who experienced the way they learnt about the acqi sition as a dramatic moment. The dominant feeling was a sense of dis-illusionment and betrayal, accompanied by the realization of differences in their ranks. The acq isition had somehow declared the previous organizational compromise obsolete. And by proposing a new organizational compromise, the acqi sition had provided a new framework for the previous frictions about organizing work: a framework of traditional managemente mployee negotiations, including issues of salaries, cost control, working hours, time management, and development projects, for example.

Normalizing the New Organization after the Acquisition

In an open conversation I had with Jackie, one of the editors, three words stood out that I noted in my notebook: difficult, ambiguous, and betrayal. As "the point of passage" between top management and the newsroom, this editor managed the reactions of the journalists, absorbed their feelings of disappoint-ment and their demands, and explained the founders' reasoning behind the decision. When I asked about leaving, the editor told me: "They brought me up to date right away, very early, so I couldn't think of leaving."

Feeling involved in the organization as much as the founders were, this moral engagement took departure outside the range of possible choices for Jackie. The acqi sition, perhaps in the way it was managed, put Jackie close to and yet different from the founders. Reflecting on the ambiguity introduced by the acquisition on the eqa lity or ineq ality of the organizational members, Jackie reflected: "We are all the same, but we are not."

As the ownership changed, the organizational compromise that arranged the conciliation between editorial and management principles no longer held, and a moment of strong critiqe developed. Journalists who had found themselves internalizing cost constraints for the benefit of the higher common goal of *Rue89*'s independence qe stioned the degree of that commonality and started thinking of themselves as "regular" employees. Money made explicit differences between those who owned shares and those who did not, between the founders and the others, between those who were there at the beginning and those who were not. As majority owners of the company's capital, the founders took the majority of the capital gain from the change of ownership. Those who had joined *Rue89* in the first months and volunteered at the start of the website had become employees of the company, "The Inhabitants of *Rue89*" that owned a small percentage of *Rue89*. With the acqi sition, they received a capital gain on a scale of a few thousand EUR, but the rest of the journalists did not. Like one of the founders, some of the Inhabitants were no longer working at *Rue89*, but had kept their shareholder status, and according to capitalist rules were worthy of receiving compensation for the risk they had taken by investing in the start-up.

The material and monetary realization of all these differences had an impact on the way in which journalists at *Rue89* were approaching work and understanding their role. Maxime talked about what she considered her disinvestment in the organization:

> I'm happy [about the acqi sition]. I feel less guilty about my recent disinvestment in *Rue89*. People who received money were blamed for the money. There were tensions, but they were adjusted within two weeks. (Fieldnotes, conversation with Maxime, April 2012)

The journalists in the newsroom seem unanimous in lamenting the way the acqi sition had been presented and the feeling of hypocrisy it engendered. The message expressed by the founders was one of satisfaction for the deal and of eqa lity for all organizational members.

Another journalist told me that the founders explained that they were divided amongst themselves. Some thought it was good, others thought it was not good, but they all agreed that it was better to sell than to downsize. The journalists agreed with this judgment, but, as Yannick said:

> We would have wanted them to take our interests into account better. They do not understand the extent to which we are involved and how hard we work. Perhaps there is the same engagement at *Libé*, but otherwise nobody else works in this way. I want a life. (Fieldnotes, conversation with Yannick, April 2012)

Given the small compensation for the journalists, they felt that the new owner had tricked the founders into a deal that was not convenient for the employees. This fed the feeling that *Rue89* was the founders' toy and that those working and contributing to its value had not been considered.

During a visit at the beginning of March, the journalists told me that right after the acquisition, overwhelmed by their feelings of disappointment, they had threatened to strike. On 22 December, the day after the public announcement was published on the website and the press release was sent out, they spent half a day together in the café down the street to discuss what to do.

The newsroom was then empty, except for management. They decided not to strike, but they had a list of clear demands they wanted the founders to take into negotiations with the buyer. Their primary demands related to improvement of salary, benefits, and such working conditions as having a company mobile phone.

And they also agreed on the urgency of having an official representative of the journalists to negotiate with the management and ownership of the company. In the first years, there had been a journalist acting as a representative, although that person's role was defined qi te loosely. Since that journalist left, no substitute had been elected, and no official union committee had ever existed in the company.

With these demands, the journalists started feeling for the first time like they were regular employees. The private engagement that had characterized the initial phase of the project, when they were sitting in the kitchen of one of the founders, did not fit the new organizational compromise under negotiation. Normalization and professionalism were words that many of them associated with the post-acqi sition phase. The change in ownership was, on the one hand, the end of a dream, a utopia, as many employees put it, and, on the other hand, a relief for being allowed to feel like normal employees in a normal relationship with their employer, including, for example, freedom to ask for a paid mobile phone, for vacation, for reimbursement of expenses.

At the beginning of January 2012, Claude Perdriel, owner of *Le Nouvel Observateur*, and by then 85 years old and the new owner of *Rue89*, visited *Rue89*'s newsroom to meet the team and welcome them into the group. The team was qi te skeptical before the meeting, but apparently became somewhat convinced during the ensuing discussion.

Independence was at the core of Perdriel's speech. He assured the team that *Rue89*'s independence would be strictly guaranteed and respected, as specifically affirmed in the contract that had been drawn up for the acqi sition of the website. As Pierre Haski wrote in a post of *Le blog du making of*: "The two teams [*Rue89* and *Le Nouvel Observateur*] have the same fierce drive of independence" (Haski, 2012).

At the press conference held the following day, the managing director of *Le Nouvel Observateur* explained the economic rationale of the acqi sition by arguing that the representatives of the company want to be as big as possible. The entrance of *Rue89* into *Le Nouvel Observateur* group made the group competitive with the other two biggest media group in France: *Le Monde* and *Le Figaro*, which was a significant issue for the advertising market.

Disappointing the Agreement

The new organizational compromise implied different qa lifications and engagements at the new *Rue89*: The founders had ceased being entrepreneurs, journalists had become employees, and *Rue89* was a subsidiary of a larger media group. Life in the newsroom after the acqi sition seemed to have found a new rhythm and a new balance. In the first six months of 2012, everyone was focused on the political elections that would take place between the end of April and the beginning of May. These were significant times not only journalistically, but also organizationally, as it had been precisely on the day of Sarkozy's election in 2007 that *Rue89* was launched.

In the beginning, exchanges between the new owner and the old founders "were great", as one of them recalled in an interview. The new owner would call them to ask how it was going and to learn things. In practice, the new organizational agreement meant that the founders of *Rue89* needed to sit in meetings with other managers in the group and to act within the larger bureaucratic structure that a big organization implies. One of them recalled a certain degree of resistance from others within the group to learn from the *Rue89* experience. The advertising team was rapidly moved to the headqa rters of *Rue89* and joined the rest of *Le Nouvel Observateur*'s advertising department, while *Rue89*'s journalistic operations seem to be left untouched.

It was a little bit more than a year after the acqi sition, the founders recalled, that the trouble started. In particular, two critical moments seem to have left significant traces in the organization. The first happened at the end of 2012 and concerned the membership of *Rue89* in the Association for the Independent Online Press (Spiil). At the end of 2012, just before Christmas, a member of the *Rue89* management team was called to a meeting with Claude Perdriel and another top manager at *Le Nouvel Observateur* Group. The *Rue89* manager thought that this was a Merry-Christmas, end-of-the-year meeting but soon realized that there was another specific aim. In the autumn of 2012, the Spiil had signed and published a manifesto for a new ecosystem of the digital press, in which it suggested a suppression of current direct subsidies to the print press. As a founding member of Spiil, *Rue89* supported and promoted this manifesto as did all the other pure-player members of the association. At that meeting, however, it became clear that the new owner, whose flagship product was a printed magazine, framed the *Rue89* membership in Spiil as a conflict of interest, as they could not be part of a printed press group while being a member of an association that wanted to cut their state financing.

In an interview in January 2017, the founder of *Rue89* recalled his first shock and realization that things were going to change for *Rue89*. On the same day, *Rue89* sent a letter to Maurice Botbol, President of Spiil, announcing *Rue89*'s resignation from the association:

> Dear friends of the Spiil,
> Upon the demand of its owner, who wishes to ensure consistency of *Rue89* with its new situation within *Le Nouvel Observateur* Group, *Rue89* leaves the Spiil as of the 1st of January 2013.
> The founders of *Rue89* join me in renewing their friendship to the members of the Spiil, a federation that they have helped create and develop and, in particular, to the member of the Bureau [leadership team], with whom fertile work has been accomplished throughout these common years.
> They remain loyal to the values that connect the members of this community of journalists and entrepreneurs and will continue being inspired by them in their future actions.
> Amicably,
> Pierre Haski,
> President of *Rue89*

At the beginning of January, then, the Spiil published an article on its website announcing the departure of *Rue89* from the federation and expressing its regret for this decision and *Rue89* announced the same thing on its website that day. Pierre Haski linked this announcement to the independence of *Rue89*, by explaining:

> This decision to qi t the professional federation does not at all concern the editorial independence of *Rue89*, which is guaranteed by the agreements signed in December 2011 and which have been scrupulously respected since then. (Haski, 2013)

Although editorial independence was guaranteed, doubts and frustration arose with this incident.

Another conflict within the new organizational compromise occurred about a year later, in December 2013. It concerned the *Rue89* logo. Until then, the layout and the graphic identity of *Rue89* had remained the same as it had been before the acqi sition. On the evening of 5 December 2013, however, the top of the website changed in a way that the journalists considered regrettable. The *Rue89* logo shrank in size and was positioned as an attachment to a larger *Le Nouvel Obs* logo. The URL of the website had also been modified from www .rue89.com to www.rue89.nouvelobs.com. This change had been justified by *Le Nouvel Observateur*'s top management as necessary; it would allow them to count the *Rue89* audience within the overall audience of the group in the official measurements of the media measurement agency, Médiamétrie.[7]

---

[7]   Médiamétrie is the leading company for media audience measurement in France. Measuring media audience is important not only to recognize the popularity of each media outlet, but also to sell and price advertising on different media outlet.

Combining the audience figures of the entire website within the group would give the group a better competitive position in the advertising market.

After "three days in which all the *Rue89* team had engaged in arm wrestling with the top management of the group", the leading team at *Rue89* finally accepted "the conditions imposed by *Le Nouvel Observateur*" (Sourdès, 2013). Thus, the logo and the URL were changed. As this decision was made, the newsroom members at *Rue89* declared a striket— he first strike in the life of *Rue89*. In the text announcing it, they explained their disappointment with this decision, "because it sacrifices our Rue" (Sourdès, 2013).

Because it was important for the journalists to communicate with their readers about the strike, they created a Reve89 logo; it means Dream89 and is wordplay with the name "*Rue89*". The journalists opened a Facebook page and launched a simple website to keep a diary of the strike. Readers commented on their updates, both on the website and on Facebook, and one of them even launched a petition under the heading "Saving *Rue89*!". It collected 671 signatures. The strike lasted for five days: The top of the website was not modified, but some concessions were made in terms of recruitment for *Rue89*.

THE END

"This is the end", said a *Rue89* journalist when we met in January 2017. By then the website had become one of the sections of *Le Nouvel Observateur*, and its editorial focus had changed, after an analysis of all the brands and their identities at the group level. At the beginning of 2014, *Le Nouvel Observateur* had itself been acqi red by the so-called BNP trio, which included business people Pierre Bergé, Xavier Niel, and Matthieu Pigasse, owners of *Le Monde Libre*, the holding company of the prestigious newspaper *Le Monde*. A few months after this acqi sition, in October 2014, following efforts to reorganize the entire galaxy of websites belonging to the Bergé, Niel, and Pigasse, *Rue89* changed its editorial line and started dedicating its journalistic efforts to investigate two subjects: new technologies and the so-called connected lifet— he societal and personal conseqe nces of new technologies.

This change in editorial focus had been met with resistance and confusion by the *Rue89* team. They had once covered general news, with a particular passion for politics and society, but were now to center their reporting on technologies and connected lifea— change that was perceived as a restriction of their journalistic freedom and impact. This change had been presented by the management team of the group as a way of clarifying its contribution to the editorial offering of the group, to specify the audience so that it would not cannibalize other news products, and to make it easier to sell to advertisers.

The participatory aspect of the website, which had been extremely important at the birth of the project in order to define the new journalism, was also downplayed over the years after the first and second acqi sition. When *Rue89* moved to the technological platform used by *Le Nouvel Observateur*, the group had outsourced moderation to a supplier, the comment section was inaccessible to the journalists, and they were no longer allowed to moderate comments. Moreover, the group had another website, *Le Plus*, the only focus of which was reader participation in news production. In a conversation in which they reported the reasoning from the group's top management, several *Rue89* journalists told me that the participatory practices they had developed risked being cannibalized and duplicated.

The changes in editorial focus were also accompanied by changes in the workforce at *Rue89*. At the beginning of 2017, after several downsizings, *Rue89* consisted of four journalists and one editor and had become a news section like many others, responding to the website editorial team. All the founders had left the website, although one of them continued to work for the group. All the journalists from the initial kitchen meetings had also left. In the spring of 2011, one of the editors said that *Rue89* was like a snake changing its skin. In 2017, the old skin was gone, but this time, unlike snakes and unlike the spring of 2011, it was not because the snake had grown.

Transformation of the organizational compromise sustaining *Rue89* as a journalistic and entrepreneurial project after its acqi sition by *Le Nouvel Observateur* testifies to a larger transformation of the way in which journalism and the news field are organized and an increasing concentration of ownership. In a review of Jacqe line Remy's (2014) book for the 50th anniversary of *Le Nouvel Observateur*, Blandine Grosjean, former vice-editor-in-chief of *Rue89*, summarizes the transformation of the press:

> Principle of reality, of marketing, of the necessity of selling (the cover pages on back pain, real estate, food that makes one younger), of the change in reading habits, of the rise of the Web, whereas this publication [*Le Nouvel Observateur*] had been wanted, invented, and conceived of, to talk about what seemed worthy of interest to the publication [to the newsroom].
>
> Nothing at *Le Nouvel Observateur* was ever conducted according to common sense, and it is for this reason that the weekly has sometimes produced genius journalism, a place where one could professionally blossom, but also stagnate, "a family" which never really abandons its own members, as those who felt like insiders liked to repeat. (Grosjean, 2014)

The founders of *Rue89*, and probably many of the journalists of the founders' persuasion, believed that the acqi sition by *Le Nouvel Observateur*, with its intellectual aura and kind owner, would defend editorial independence and guarantee the long-term value of *Rue89*. This turned out to be their highway into larger transformations of the media landscape in France and in Europe, and little could the promises of defending them hold. To my surprise, this is where the Swedish story of *Göteborgs-Posten* and Stampen, full of pragmatism and business sense, intersects my French story of *Rue89*—n organization that overwhelmed and pleasantly seduced me for its idealism and sincere commitment to journalism.

6. Compromising in the name of independence

> In old days men had the rack. Now they have the Press. That is an improvement certainly. But still it is very bad, and wrong, and demoralizing. Somebodyw— as it Burke?e— alled journalism the fourth estate. That was true at the time no doubt. But at the present moment it is the only estate. It has eaten up the other three. The Lords Temporal say nothing, the Lords Spiritual have nothing to say, and the House of Commons has nothing to say and says it. We are dominated by Journalism. (Wilde, 1891/1998)

The stories in this book addresses the ways in which independence has been organized and practiced in three European news companies. Despite their different locations, sizes, and ages, theses employees shared a belief in traditional journalism and attempted to adapt it to the brave new world of news production. Like many other media workers, they understood themselves to be playing two distinctly different and often contradictory roles: (1) serving the public interest "by supplying information, opinion, and diversion, and by facilitating the social interactions that are vital to the functioning of society and democratic institutions" and (2) acting as "economic actors that create, produce, market, and distribute their products in a commercial marketplace" (Picard, 2005, p. 337). My studies revealed many of the tensions between these two roles and the changes made and remade in everyday organizational life— all in the name of independence of what Julianne Schultz called the "Bastard Estate" (Schultz, 1998, p. 4).

Despite often being discussed in light of new technological and economic conditions, media independence seems to be generally understood as inevitably intertwined with a free market enterprise (Bollier, 2001; Glasser & Gunther, 2005). The three newspapers analyzed in this book represent three cases of organizational compromise between journalism and management, with changes occurring during the time of my study. As the field studies demonstrate, these compromises were organizational in a double sense of the word: They consisted of the organizing of activities, things, and ideas around news production, but they were also created by an organization, carried traces of its history, and were influenced by trends in its organizational field.

At *Il Sole-24 Ore*, I summarized the compromise between journalism and management as "money versus news". Independence at this Italian financial newspaper, owned by the National Federation of Employers, was translated into a fierce defense of journalistic autonomy, materialized in the separation of activities, spaces, and ideas related to journalism from those related to managementt— he Newsroom vs. the Business. The story of *Il Sole-24 Ore* tells how professional autonomy was organized and practiced over a decade ago and, more specifically, how it was then defended and renegotiated around the websites, particularly in light of the project of integrating newspaper and website production in 20072008. Money—making it or saving itt— endered everything worthwhile on the Business side of the enterprise. The highest principle of worth in the Newsroom, on the other hand was news of qa lity and the impact it generated.

In 2011 I began my study of *Göteborgs-Posten*, in the second biggest Swedish city of Gothenburg, where I live. I was surprised to find neither the inflamed fights between journalism and management nor the idealistic defense of journalistic reasoning against commercial principles. Rather, I found a generally agreed-upon and pragmatic compromise between journalism and management, which I summarized as "making news for money". There were, indeed, stories from the past describing flaming discussions in meetings of journalists and managers, but these alleged events, it seems, had been replaced by the pragmatic understanding that money is needed in order to survive. The most important asset that could be monetized was the newspaper's credibility vis-à-vis the local community, especially in light of the new possibilities introduced by the webf— ree information and non-journalistic competition, for example. These opportunities were accompanied (caused by?) diminishing advertising revenues and a decreasing readership, especially among young people. This story, which appeared well-rehearsed, was also used to frame the multiple acqi sitions of *Göteborgs-Posten*'s holding company, Stampen, and the aggregation of many local newspapers into a large media group. At the Swedish local media group, independence was translated into a relentless contest for a growing portion of the local news market both in the local region and in a growing number of regions, and for improved profitability across those regions. The construction of Stampen, however, which was justified as a way of increasing the money made by selling news, did not function for long after my first visit to *Göteborgs-Posten*: It did not fulfill the hope of creating synergy in the organization, and it did not serve as a profit-making machine. Money made by selling news was lost in attempts to make even more money by acqi ring many local newspapers.

While I was approaching the Swedish newspaper, I was already beginning my study of *Rue89* in France. Coming from my experience at *Il Sole-24 Ore* and comparing it with my first contacts with *Göteborgs-Posten*, my time at *Rue89* was liberating, because the people I interviewed there expressed hope for journalism and democracy and faith in their ideals. At *Rue89*, I could recognize both the passionate frictions between journalism and management

I had experienced at *Il Sole-24 Ore* and the pragmatic realization that news is a business, which I had heard at *Göteborgs-Posten*.

Between 2011 and 2012, I studied the French pioneering participatory news website, *Rue89*. Its organizational compromise at the time of my field immersion was "making money for news", and I traced this compromise back in time to the start of the project and outside the boundaries of the organization. *Rue89* had translated independence into a strenuous search for sources of income, in order to finance the core of the enterprise: journalism. This organizational compromise that the founders and the journalists tried fiercely to defend and patiently to actualize did not take hold, however, in the form I had encountered it. A friendly magazine company bought the enterprise, then resold it a couple of years later to a larger media group. During this shift of ownership, management performed a strategic cleaning of the website portfolio, revising *Rue89*'s editorial line into smaller coverage and a cost-saving package. This move resulted in many employees leaving the company more or less voluntarily and others being relocated within the larger company. "This was the end"t— he end of the original compromisea— s many interlocutors told me in January 2017, five years after the sale of *Rue89* and my immersive study period at the news website.

These three cases lead to my interpretation of media independence as an organizational process of compromise between journalism and management. This compromise temporarily settled conflicts between democracy and profitbot h principles of worths— ettlements that were necessary for making news. Such compromises betrayed yet simultaneously actualized the ideal of independence that justified them. Whether one is for (news for money), against (news vs. money), or supported by (money for news) money-making, the making of news may look similar at different times and places, as Czarniawska's (2011) studies in news agencies also showed. In critical situations, however, the conflicts and subseqe nt adjustments differ, and the overarching ideal of independence as an uncontestable keyword may have to be used in different ways to settle disagreements (Czarniawska, 1988). Through disagreements, agreements and compromises around the making of news, my studies show how media independence is made a matter that matters (Latour, 2005a).

Despite the various interpretations of independence and the different seqe nces of compromises reached to realize it, I was struck by the fact that there were three common aspects of the process of compromising in the name of independence. (1) Participants in the process of compromising could easily switch from the defense of one principle to the defense of another. Journalists did not necessarily defend democracy, and managers did not necessarily argue on the side of cost saving and increased profits. (2) Compromises were put to work through inscriptions into artifactsm— aterial like newspapers and websites or linguistics like the labels "journalist-entrepreneurs" or "local media group". By "inscription", I refer here to the process by which rules and norms are incorporated into the design of material artifacts (technical inscription) and the composition of language expressions (literary inscriptions) (Joerges & Czarniawska, 1998; Czarniawska, 2008). Latour and Woolgar (1979) discovered the scientists in laboratories intensely occupied with inscribing the world around them rather than mirroring it and Joerges and Czarniawska (1998) showed how technology is rife with inscriptions made by organizations and about organizations. The inscriptions of compromises in the organizations I studied carry traces of past conflicts and their resolutions. Although helping to carry the compromise forward, they are fragile and exposed to critiqe , negotiation, and re-inscripting. (3) The recurring tests, critical moments, and subseqe nt fragile compromises make independence durable, but not stable. In the next three sections, I address these common aspects of compromising in the name of independence.

VARIED ASSEMBLAGES

My studies have demonstrated that the organizational compromises between journalism and management do not necessarily imply negotiations between groups of people representing one or the other principle of worth. Neither are such compromises objects, statically carrying and representing the idea of a common good, such as democracy or profit. People and things are not divided into competing teams, but constantly move within and outside news organizations and their compromises in the name of independence, much like people and things of Boltanski and Thévenot's (2006) world of worth-making and justification. People and things can therefore be categorized in different ways and used differently in the same situation (Thévenot, 2001).

My interlocutors were not always restricted to one role; at any one time they could have been journalists, employees, entrepreneurs, readers, editors, managers. In the critical situations I analyzed, the same person could play different roles in both different and similar situationsa– mutability that might have invited self-criticism and doubt over their past decisions. In *Il Sole-24 Ore*, journalists and managers seemed to be relatively stable tribes, actively performing boundary work to keep their roles distinct, thus speaking and acting on behalf of a given principle of worth. I did not observe this phenomenon at *Göteborgs-Posten*/Stampen or at *Rue89*. At *Göteborgs-Posten*, however, many journalists remembered a time when the wall was solid between the newsroom and management, even between marketing and advertising rooms. But they talked about the contemporary necessity of embracing cost-saving and income-making concerns and the need to contribute to the company's profitability. At *Rue89*, the mutability of positions in relation to journalism and management as frames of worth was visible in practice. Ideas and actions for business and editorial developments at *Rue89* were tested both in journalistic and management terms. If a compromise were to be reached, such ideas needed to be righti— n terms of their contribution to democracy and in their ability to save costs or increase revenues.

As Mary Douglas (1986) noted over three decades ago, society is ordered by institutional categories, such as journalism and management, money and news, democracy and profit, and this classifying work has been "already done for us" (Douglas, 1986, p. 100). The studies I presented in this book show how, in the midst of technological change and an increasing plurality of media, these categories were still mobilized by my interlocutors, both to classify people and things and to defend against criticism. As many scholars have shown (see, e.g., Bowker & Star, 2000), classifications are neither neutral nor natural, but rather are political processes involving judgment. The founders of *Rue89*, for example, would sometimes classify themselves as journalists and sometimes as entrepreneurs, employers, or journalist-entrepreneurs. By doing so, they could legitimately act differently in different or even similar situations, and always in the name of independence. Professional judgment and discretion are therefore involved in the act of classifying something or somebody, as speaking and acting for journalism or management, democracy or profit. This judgment can be exposed to criticism: Can the founders of *Rue89* really still qa lify as journalists after having started an enterprise? Can they really make the best decisions for long-term profits, given that they have been working as journalists all their lives? Is the choice to publish a magazine a good one for democracy, given that it strains the newsroom's journalists?

INSCRIPTIONS ONTO ARTIFACTS

Compromises between journalism and management are realized through inscriptions onto material and linguistic artifacts (Joerges & Czarniawska, 1998). These artifacts are produced by organizational personnel who assemble different elements into relatively stable compositions. The composite character of these artifacts onto which compromises between journalism and management are inscribed renders them fragile, however, as they carry traces of different principles of worth and critical moments, which could be easily recalled from these reminders.

The stories of everyday life at *Il Sole-24 Ore* demonstrate how fragile is the composition of print and online news products as daily objects of compromise. The placing of advertising on odd-numbered pages or the size of an advertorial section in the middle of the newspaper creates a critical moment, reminding the newsroom that the newspaper carries not only journalistic content, but also advertising. The democratic goals of journalism are constantly being tested against the commercial goals of management. The division of the website into pink and blue areas— he pink dedicated to journalism, the blue to marketing contentga ve rise to qe stions about the real meaning of journalism, and whether content that has passed through the blue area and is thereby deemed suitable for marketing can ever return to pink. The very composition of news products brings to mind the dual order of worth that characterizes news organizations. It materializes the compromise between democracy and profit, but also exposes this very compromise to further criticisms and renegotiations.

This organizing independence through the neat separation of journalism and management brings a romanticized view of journalism to mind. As Theodore Glasser and Marc Gunther (2005) wrote:

> Journalists assert their independence and autonomy by establishing, sometimes literally but usually metaphorically, certain boundaries for the profession ().. journalists build "walls"w- alls between news and advertising, between the news pages and the opinion pages, between the business of journalism and the practice of journalism, between publishers and editors. And to establish the credibility of daily news, journalists draw "lines"l- ines between facts and opinions, between description and promotion, between analysis and advocacy, between news judgments and moral judgments, between a journalist's private beliefs and the public expression of them. (p. 390)

Although the authors were referring to the US media, this qot e appropriately describes what I found at *Il Sole-24 Ore*, where the boundaries between journalism and management were inscribed, albeit more or less continuously rewritten, into physical and linguistic artifacts.

The story of *Göteborgs-Posten* and Stampen demonstrates that the linguistic artifact, "local media group", worked well in convincing the people who worked there of the appropriateness of the growth strategy chosen by the owners' family. "Local" evoked the glory of local journalism; "media" brought the newspaper into a future in which technology would render obsolete the distinctions among newspapers, Internet, and TV; and "group" emphasized the synergies achieved by acqi sitionsby sharing printing plants and content, for example. Perhaps it also created a sense of hope in a brighter future, despite the challenging times for traditional print operations. The overall design of Stampen as a local media group was recurrently justified by various platitudes, like "if you don't eat, you are eaten", as the company's owner, Peter Hjö ne, said on several occasions, and "we need to strengthen our own capacity so that we would not be swept away by the wind of the big players", as CEO Tomas Brunegård put it. Such platitudes conventionalized what needed to be done, so that Stampen could maintain independence. They established the normality of producing news for making money, and reduced tensions by universalizing survival through commercial success as the common ground of the organization. *Göteborgs-Posten*'s framing of independence echoes the wisdom of media economists. As Robert Picard (2005) said of developments in the US media companies:

> Historically, media firms tended to be small- and medium-size enterprises that produced steady incomes for their owners and provided regular returns beyond the costs of their operations. During the second half of the twentieth century, the progressive growth of advertising expenditures in the United States increased those returns significantly, turning media companies into investment vehicles and increasing the economic and commercial pressures on media firms. ().. [F]inancially successful media companies have the resources to serve social needs and be more independent of outside pressures over time than less financially secure firms. (p. 339)

This qot e reads like a summary of how independence was discussed and strived for at *Göteborgs-Posten* and Stampen. Perhaps it is not an accident that the CEO and top management team leading the company at the time of the study made recurrent trips to the USA (Westgårdh & Johnsson, 2012).

At *Rue89*, a large number of labels like "pure players", "independent online news producers", "participatory media", " PORSCHE", "journalist-entrepreneurs", and "entrepreneurial journalism", has been used to describe what *Rue89* stood for. Many of these labels were composite, as they juxtaposed other labels referring to different principles of worth and actions. "Independent online news producers", for example, was the label created and used by a group of journalists who had started their own companies to produce and distribute news online: "Independent" referred to the fact that they were not owned by large and powerful groups; "online" was opposed to traditional media, like print and TV, and signaled a certain innovative culture; "news" anchored them to a well-known category of content and to the journalistic profession; and "producers" evoked the association with a product that needed to be sold on the market in order to generate a profit. *Rue89* actively contributed to the establishment of the label "independent online news producers" in France by participating with other organizations in the founding of a lobbying and trade association, the French Association for Independent Online News Producers (Spiil). This composite label was particularly powerful in the organization as the carrier of a compromise between journalism and management that was perceived as a "revolution" and as common to an entire category of actors in the news field.

As the stories in Chapters 4 and 5 demonstrate, tensions arose recurrently in response to criticism over the appropriateness of actions taken in order to finance news, but these tensions were constantly reduced and settled by pointing to the common ground. The founders made well-rehearsed generalizations that tended to ease critical moments and establish the normality of local compromises in the name of independence. "We are all in the same boat." "We are journalists, so we understand you [young journalists]." "We need to reach breakeven in order to be editorially independent."

Labels categorize the world and are performative, as they have implications for what people do (Douglas, 1986; Czarniawska, 1988). Once labels are established, Mary Douglas (1986) argued, they have a stabilizing effect on the "flux of social life, and even create to some extent the realities to which they apply" (p. 101). Labels, like objects, make society durable, via a dynamic process that she described:

> The relation between people and the things they name is never static. ().. Naming is only one set of inputs; it is on the surface of the classification process. The interaction that Hacking describes goes round, from people making institutions to institutions making classifications, to classifications entailing actions, to actions calling for names, and to people and other living creatures responding to the naming, positively and negatively. (p. 101)

LASTING FRAGILITY

The third common aspect of the three cases I studied is the temporary nature of their compromises between journalism and management, inscribed in composite artifacts. The fragility of these compromises was seen in the criticism of readers and of those who worked in the organizations. The heterogeneous composition of the artifacts invited criticism, but these critiqes usually sounded reformistic, and those involved in critical incidents seemed to be able to settle them with help of an established label and a rehearsed platitude. Yet at times their frustration, rather than reducing uncertainty, was greeted with platitudes that did not serve to mitigate the problem. Stories of Stampen's bankruptcy and *Rue89*'s double sale demonstrate the unfolding of radically critical moments, when the labels no longer connected to things and experiences. The crises were resolved by new compromises, which had to be inscribed into new labels and new platitudes.

Within Stampen, the composite label "local media group" and the associated platitudes functioned well at first to reduce tensions and create a common ground, but did not long convince bankers, readers, or employees. They started "produc[ing] irritation rather than facilitation" (Czarniawska, 1988), and the whole compromise apparently achieved via the construction of the local media group was put to the test and criticized. At *Rue89*, composite labels pointing to the blending of journalism and management through entrepreneurship and the accompanying platitudes no longer functioned as compromising devices when *Rue89* was sold. There was increasing doubt about the meaning of those linguistic artifacts and the correctness of the structure of action they projected (Czarniawska, 1988). Thus many employees left, and those who remained created a new compromise by leaving business management in the hands of the new owners and managers and trying to focus on traditional editorial work.

The world of news making portrayed in this book, thus, is full of objects that, as Latour put it (2005b, p. 20), are "variegated, uncertain, complicated, far reaching, heterogeneous, risky, historical, local, material and networky". Although I have observed unq estioned matters of fact being acted upon in the making of news, my stories here have focused on moments in which those objects and the compromises they carry show fragility and assemble people that disagree to come to "some sort of provisional makeshift (dis)agreement" (Latour, 2005b, p. 23).

FOLLOWING NEW ARTEFACTS

Quite a few years have passed since the stories portrayed in this book were being played out. Many say that the world has totally changed: We are now post-Trump, post-Cambridge Analytica, post-COVID-19a– nd also post-truth, post-democracy, and even post-algorithm. Although I agree that new political and company leaders have introduced new vocabularies and sometimes new practices into the light of the public sphere, many issuesl– ike media independenceha ve not been swept away by political, societal, and technological change. After a pause of some years in my fieldwork, I returned to it in 2017 and, indulging my interest in technology and societal fashions, I started by following one of the hottest contemporary technological trends: robots and Artificial Intelligence (AI) in the media.

I was especially interested in the label "robotjournalism", and I soon found many other neologisms in media vocabulary: datajournalism, data-driven journalism, AI-enhanced journalism, automated journalism, algorithmic journalism, machine journalism, social news verification. I also encountered many new technological tools that seemed to be common among practitioners and reminded me of my outsider's role: Slack, Google Hangouts, Zoom, Google-inverted search, Python. Although I had previously heard many voices joining Evgeny Morozov's (2012) concerns about a robot stealing his Pulitzer Prize, the anticipation of dystopic scenarios for public debate and democracy and my study of robots and AI in the news production field has brought me to new places and new people. I left the people, places, and websites described in this book with a feeling of sadness over the inevitable inertia dragging down news organizations. The development of the cases presented in this book corresponded to what many other scholars have noted. (See, e.g., Järventie-Thesleff et al., 2014; Lehtisaari et al., 2018.)

> … [b]esides a number of countries in Asia, in most continents the majority of countries continue to experience a dated business model of commercial news media that

has been broken for some time. Large numbers of news publishers have substantially downsized their operations. Many have filed for bankruptcy or been dissolved into existing companies. (Bélair-Gagnon et al., 2019, p. 2)

But I have also found a great deal of entrepreneurial enthusiasm and experiments in new organizations, most of them linked to new technological possibilities. This realization reminded me in some ways of *Rue89*: There are hopes for the ability of new technologies to remedy the bad practices of traditional media; there are the efforts of innovating journalists, together with the incessant search for financing, talk about business models, and dreams of a breakeven.

Media scholars have described these new organizations and projects as *peripheral actors* (Grafström & Windell, 2012; Eldridge, 2017; Bélair-Gagnon & Holton, 2018a), as "a particular group of professionals who incorporate new organizational forms and experimental practice in pursuit of redefining the field and its structural foundations" (Hepp & Loosen, 2021, p. 578). Bélair-Gagnon and Holton (2018b) have called these peripheral actors "journalistic strangers", evoking Georg Simmel's notion of a stranger as somebody "who has not belonged [to the group] from the beginning" and "imports qa lities into it which do not and cannot stem from the group itself" (Simmel, 1950, p. 402, cited in Bélair-Gagnon & Holton, 2018b, p. 72).

FINDING NEW ORGANIZATIONS

Although my colleagues studying robots in healthcare found impressive and gigantic machines able to scan the body, even diagnose it and operate on it, my search for robots and AI in the news field was in line with the observation of Finnish media scholars Carl-Gustav Lindén and Hanna Tuulonen (2019) in their report for WAN-IFRA (World Association of Newspapers): "AI has a hype problem and we need to put aside our Hollywood-inspired ideas about super-advanced AI and instead see the automation process as a logical extension of the Industrial Revolution" (p. 5). Yet I have encountered many entrepreneurs who are experimenting with new models for organizing work and making money. Three examples are particularly noteworthy: the platform model, the AI company model, and the interorganizational collaboration model.

In the *platform model*, anything published by individual writers is their own responsibility, for which they receive their own reward. Successful platforms in other fields, like Spotify and Netflix, provide inspiration for this model in journalism. The company owning the platform does not usually have either an editorial role or publishing responsibility, like it would in a traditional newspaper. These roles and responsibilities are left to the individual journalist, whereas the company provides technology and sometimes shares income with the writers. These writers are not necessarily journalists; they can be academics and consultants, for example— nyone who wants to reach a public audience. This is the case with *The Conversation Canada*, the Swedish *Gazzine*, and the more broadly read US *Medium*.

With the *AI company model*, the primary goals are the development of an intelligent system and its training on news data.[1] Income often comes from offering services based on the AI system to other organizations, although it may be used for purposes other than publishing news. Here the collaboration between the often-reduced editorial stafft— echnology replaces part of the journalistic work, after alla— nd various AI specialists, like annotators, programmers, and data scientists is crucial to the design and implementation of the system. This is the case of *Logically* in the UK, *Journalism Plus Plus* in Sweden, and perhaps *Deepnews.ai* in the USA.

The *interorganizational collaboration model* for social innovation in news features representatives from a heterogeneous group of organizations and professions, building more or less temporary cooperation on issues that may be difficult to tackle separately. Such collaborations often have composite financing as their basis—funding from big technology companies, like Google, Facebook, or Microsoft. That is the case for *Electionland* and *First Draft* in the USA, *Pop-up Newsroom* in the UK, *Faktiskt* in Norway, and *Belling Cats* in the Netherlands.

Scholarly attention has been focused on the individual motivations, identity, and norms of entrepreneurs, journalists, and technicians working as peripheral actors (Belair-Gagnon & Holton, 2018a). The very process of organizing these new initiatives has been overlooked, however, whether these initiatives are defined as interlopers, strangers, or peripherals, and rarely has their way of translating and practicing the idea of (media) independence been an object of investigation. Vos and Singer (2016) and Hermida and Young (2019) provide two exceptions. Here, I use the three observations on the process of compromising in the name of independence to reflect on possible new ways of organizing independence in these new organizational forms.

1. *Increasingly mutable assemblages.* It seems that the group of professionals populating the new news initiatives is increasingly heterogeneous. Apart from journalists and managers, there are programmers, interactions designers, technicians, activists, consultants, and researchers. Organizational affiliation also seems to be increasingly heterogeneous.

---

[1] AI jargon refers to "training on AI data", meaning that an intelligent system uses some data to learn and improve the probability of its prediction success.

These people are employees in big and small companies, founders of more or less successful enterprises, members of foundations, project contractors, or freelancers, sometimes playing several of these roles simultaneously.

Media scholars have primarily focused on individual motivations, but little is known about the process of daily negotiations and compromise among various ways of valuing work. Many of those "strangers" are not peripheral to journalism in their experience and education, but they have worked with business management and technology. They may be liminal to all of those areas but may also travel to the center of the world of journalism, management, technology, and civic activism; they may defend the principles of each of those worlds and feel perfectly at ease in all their languages.

2. *Old sayings are controlling new artifacts.* In the current discourse in the field, I have recognized two main justifications of the efforts to increase the use of automation technologies: that automation saves money and that it allows journalists to do what is really "the core of their work"—that which they most enjoy doing. This reasoning was perhaps most visible at *Göteborgs-Posten*, where I had observed attempts to increase the number of automated tasks, especially in editing and publishing items on several platforms and hearing journalists and editors expressing their desire to automate tasks that were considered boring and unworthy of human effort. Not only was automation supposed to free journalists to work at what they really want to do and save money; it would allow them to end their working day at a decent time.

    What struck me then and continues to intrigue me is this "core" of journalism. In fact, computer programs can now, more or less intelligently, get articles published in a timely fashion and edit the headlines to fit the medium on which they are read, whether computer, mobile, tablet, or newspaper. They can also write texts, prioritize news for the homepage, recommend a suitable selection of articles for a reader, find statistical patterns and variations in a large data set, verify the authenticity of photographs, and perform a number of other tasks that used to be done by humans. As the stories in this book demonstrate, some of these tasks—like the prioritizing of news described in Chapter 2—used to be a time-consuming task reqiring great professional skill and effort.

    Yet another justification for the use of automation technology was the possibility of covering things in new ways and performing tasks that would be impossible to perform manually. Investigative datajournalism—the systematic and often automated investigation of big data sources—serves as a good example. Automation allows for the visual interactive representation of the investigation results, for the personalizing of content selection at the level of the individual reader, and even for optimizing the number of articles to be published at the optimal time in order to maximize income.

3. *Fragile paying out.* Overall, the most striking difference I noticed during my return to the field was the enthusiasm and hope for the future of news and its relevance. In the wake of President Trump's election, the Cambridge Analytica scandal, and the outbreak of the COVID-19 pandemic, there seems to be a reinforced belief in the importance of journalism in democracy, and the necessity of its independence. This situation has evolved despite the seemingly increasing difficulty of financing news production in a stable way. Many new initiatives in the news field all over the world are financed by philanthropic foundations and dedicated funds from technology giants, like the Google News Initiatives, Facebook News Fund, and Microsoft. This funding is often temporary and project-based and must be negotiated project by project. It is indeed ironic that much of the renewal in the news field is financed by those that have long been considered enemies. But perhaps this is not strange, considering the mutable careers of those peripheral actors.

REFRAMING INDEPENDENCE AS A PROCESS OF COMPROMISING

Although my search for robots and AI in the news field has permitted me to meet many new characters and discover new organizational forms, I have also found qe stions, conflicts, debates, and negotiations similar to those described and discussed in this book. More knowledge is certainly needed if we are to understand how independence is organized in new ways, and how compromises are being inscribed into new technology. But I want to conclude with a call for the reframing of media independence.

Rather than being a monolithic category, to which an organization may or may not subscribe in a universal, eternal, and absolute manner, my investigation of three news companies suggests that independence can be conceptualized as a continuous process of seeking compromise between the values of journalism and the values of business managementa— nd possibly among other orders of worth. This process implies friction and conflict, sometimes settled into compromises that do not hold for long, but are constantly qe stioned, may be resettled, and even fail. Such a process compromises independence, even as it actualizes it. As my doctoral advisor, Barbara Czarniawska, often says, there are not better or worse organizations, only better or worse times.

References

Aagård, Martin (2015, April 16). Stoppa stö t ill mediekungarna. *Aftonbladet*, p. 5.

Abbott, Andrew (1988). *The system of professions: An essay on the expert division of labour*. Chicago, IL: University of Chicago Press.

Achtenhagen, Leona & Raviola, Elena (2007). Organizing internal tensions: Duality management of media companies. In Achtenhagen, L. (ed.) *Organizing media: Mastering the challenges of organizational change*. Jökpi ng, Sweden: Jökpi ng International Business School Research Reports (page numbers unavailable).

Achtenhagen, Leona & Raviola, Elena (2009). Balancing tensions during convergence: Duality management in a newspaper company. *The International Journal on Media Management*, 11(1), 32–41.

ADS (2008). *Trimestrale n. 132. ADS Notizie*. Retrieved on July 25, 2021 from: https://www.adsnotizie.it/da tipos t98.asp.

af Kleen, Bjö n (2014, May 2). Vi kan tvingas minska utgivningen. *Dagens Nyheter*, pp. 7. Retrieved on July 25, 2021 from https://www.dn.se/kultur-noje/vi-kan-tvingas-minska-utgivningen/.

af Kleen, Bjö n (2014, December 25). Tidningsbaronernas sista strid. *Dagens Nyheter*, pp. 56–60. Retrieved on July 25, 2021 from https://www.dn.se/kultur-noje/tidningsbaronernas-sista-strid/.

Annisette, Marcia, & Richardson, Alan J. (2011). Justification and accounting: Applying sociology of worth to accounting research. *Accounting, Auditing & Accountability Journal*, 24(2), 229–249.

Bélair-Gagnon, Valérie, & Holton, Avery E. (2018a). Boundary work, interloper media, and analytics in newsrooms: An analysis of the roles of web analytics companies in news production. *Digital Journalism*, 6(4), 492–508.

Bélair-Gagnon, Valérie, & Holton, A. E. (2018b). Strangers to the game? Interlopers, intralopers, and shifting news production. *Media and Communication*, 6(4), 70–78.

Bélair-Gagnon, Valérie, Holton, Avery E., & Westlund, Oscar (2019). Space for the liminal. *Media and Communication*, 7(4), 1–7.

Bennett, James (2015). Introduction: The utopia of independent media: Independence, working with freedom and working for free. In Bennett, James, & Strange, Niki (eds.) *Media independence: Working with freedom or working for free*. New York: Routledge, pp. 1–28.

Bessy, Christian, & Favereau, Olivier (2003). Institutions et économie des conventions. *Cahiers D'économie Politique*, 44, 119–164.

Boczkowski, Pablo J. (2005). *Digitizing the news: Innovation in online newspapers*. Cambridge, MA: MIT Press.

Boerman, Sophie C., Helberger, Natali, van Noort, Guda, & Hoofnagle, Chris J. (2018). Sponsored blog content: What do the regulations say: and what do bloggers say. *J. Intell. Prop. Info. Tech. & Elec. Com. L.*, 9, 146.

Bollier, David (2001). The evolution of journalism in a changing market ecology. In Goldmark, Peter & Bollier, David (eds.) *Old values, new world: Harnessing the legacy of independent journalism for the future.* Washington, DC: The Aspen Institute, pp. 27–49.

Boltanski, Luc (2011). *On critique: A sociology of emancipation.* Cambridge: Polity Press.

Boltanski, Luc & Thévenot, Laurent (2006). *On justification: Economies of worth.* Princeton, NJ: Princeton University Press.

Bourdieu, Pierre (1979). *Distinction: A social critique of the judgement of taste.* Cambridge, MA: Harvard University Press.

Bourdieu, Pierre (1992/1997). *The rules of art: Genesis and structure of the artistic field.* Cambridge: Polity Press.

Bourdieu, Pierre (1996). *Sur la television.* Paris: Liber-Raisons d'Agir.

Bowker, Geoffrey C., & Star, Susan Leigh (2000). *Sorting things out: Classification and its consequences.* Cambridge, MA: MIT Press.

Briggs, Mark (2012). *Entrepreneurial journalism: How to build what's next for news.* Washington, DC: CQ Press.

Brooks, Richard (Director) (1952). *Deadline* [film]. Producer: Sol C. Siegel.

Bruno, Nicola & Nielsen, Rasmus K. (2012). *Survival is success: Journalistic online start-ups in Western Europe.* Reuters Institute for the Study of Journalism, University of Oxford. Retrieved on June 25, 2021 from: https://ora.ox.ac.uk/objects/uuid:32ff449e-dc01-49fb-b579-a7dc1c1a5c89.

Brown, Clyde, Waltzer, Herbert, & Waltzer, Miriam B. (2001). Daring to be heard: Advertorials by organized interests on the op-ed page of *The New York Times*, 1985‡ 998. *Political Communication*, 18(1), 23–50.

Cameron, Glenn T., Ju-Pak, Kuen-Hee, & Kim, Bong-Hyun (1996). Advertorials in magazines: Current use and compliance with industry guidelines. *Journalism & Mass Communication Quarterly*, 73(3), 722–733.

Carlson, Matt (2015). When news sites go native: Redefining the advertisinge ditorial divide in response to native advertising. *Journalism*, 16(7), 849–865.

Carlyle, Thomas (1837/2006). *The French revolution. A history.* Retrieved on June 22, 2021 from: https://www.gutenberg.org/files/1301/1301-h/1301-h.htm # ink2HCH0039.

Carlyle, Thomas (1893/1993). *On heroes, hero-worship, and the heroic in history* (Vol. 1). Berkley, CA: University of California Press.

Cloutier, Charlotte & Langley, Ann (2007). Competing rationalities in organizations: A theoretical and methodological overview. *Les cahiers de recherché du GéPS*, 1(3), 1–35.

Cloutier, Charlotte, & Langley, Ann. (2013). The logic of institutional logics: Insights from French pragmatist sociology. *Journal of Management Inquiry*, 22(4), 360–380.

Coddington, Mark (2014). Defending judgment and context in "original reporting": Journalists' construction of newswork in a networked age. *Journalism*, 15(6), 678–695.

Coddington, Mark (2015). The wall becomes a curtain. In Carlson, Matt, & Lewis, Seth C. (eds.) *Boundaries of journalism: Professionalism, practices and participation.* New York: Routledge, pp. 67–82.

Czarniawska, Barbara (1988). *To coin a phrase: On organizational talk, organizational control and management consulting.* Study of Power and Democracy in Sweden.

Czarniawska, Barbara (2004). On time, space, and action nets. *Organization*, 11(6), 773–791.

Czarniawska, Barbara (2008). How to misuse institutions and get away with it: Some reflections on institutional theory (ies). In Thornton, Patricia H., Ocasio, William,

Greenwood, Royston, Oliver, Christine, Suddaby, Roy & Sahlin, Kerstin (eds.) *The Sage handbook of organizational institutionalism*, London: Sage Publications, pp. 769–782.

Czarniawska, Barbara (2011). *Cyberfactories: How news agencies produce news.* Cheltenham, UK and Northampton, MA, USA: Edward Elgar Publishing.

Daigle, Pascale, & Rouleau, Linda (2010). Strategic plans in arts organizations: A tool of compromise between artistic and managerial values. *International Journal of Arts Management*, 12(3), 13–30.

Denis, Jean-Louis, Langley, Ann, & Rouleau, Linda (2007). Strategizing in pluralistic contexts: Rethinking theoretical frames. *Human Relations*, 60, 179–215.

Deqe ch, David (2005). Cognition and valuation: Some similarities and contrasts between institutional economics and the economics of conventions. *Journal of Economic Issues*, 39(2), 465–473.

Dolnick, Sam (2018). *Tapping Technology to Advance the Future of Journalism.* Retrieved on May 9, 2020 from: https://www.nytimes.com/2018/01/03/technology/personaltech/technology-future-journalism.html.

Douglas, Mary (1986). *How institutions think.* Syracuse, NY: Syracuse University Press.

Doyle, Gillian (2013). *Understanding media economics.* London: Sage Publications.

Dupuy, Jean-Pierre, Eymard-Duvernay, Francois, Favereau, Olivier, Orléan, André, Salais, Robert, & Thévenot, Laurent (1989). Introduction. *Revue économique*, 40(2), 141–145. Special Issue: 'L'économie des conventions'.

Eckman, Alyssa, & Lindlof, Tomas (2003). Negotiating the Gray Lines: An ethnographic case study of organizational conflict between advertorials and news. *Journalism Studies*, 4(1), 65–77.

Economist, The (2006). Who killed the newspaper? August 26. Retrieved on July 25, 2021 from: https://www.economist.com/leaders/2006/08/24/who-killed-the-newspaper.

Ekströn , Mats, & Westlund, Oscar (2019). The dislocation of news journalism: A conceptual framework for the study of epistemologies of digital journalism. *Media and Communication*, 7(1), 259–270.

Eldridge, Scott A. (2017). *Online journalism from the periphery: Interloper media and the journalistic field.* London: Routledge.

Engel, G. V., & Hall, R. H. (1973). The growing industrialization of the professions. In Freidson, Eliot (ed.) *The professions and their prospects.* Beverly Hills, CA: Sage Publications.

Engwall, Lars (1978). *Newspapers as organizations.* Farnborough: Saxon House.

Fagerling, Marita, & Norbäck, Maria (2005). Newsroom identities: Group configurations and transforming boundaries during the introduction of a web edition. *Intervention Research*, 1(2), 191–207.

Favereau, Olivier, Biencourt, Olivier, Eymard Duvernay, Francois (2001). *Where do markets come from? From (quality) conventions.* Paris: INSEAD.

Ferrer Conill, R. (2016). Camouflaging church as state: An exploratory study of journalism's native advertising. *Journalism Studies*, 17(7), 904–914.

Freidson, Eliot (1986). *Professional powers: A study of the institutionalization of formal knowledge.* Chicago, IL: University of Chicago Press.

Friedland, Roger O. & Alford, Robert (1991). Bringing society back in: Symbols, practices, and institutional contradictions. In DiMaggio, P., Powell, J., & Woody W. (eds.) *The new institutionalism in organizational analysis.* Chicago, IL: University of Chicago Press, pp. 232–263.

Friedman, Jeffrey (2003). Public opinion: Bringing the media back in. *Critical Review*, 15(3–4), 239–260.

Fronda, Yannick & Moriceau, Jean-Luc (2008). I am not your hero: Change management and culture shocks in a public sector corporation. *Journal of Organizational Change Management*, 21, 589–609.

Glasser, Theodor L., & Gunther, Marc (2005). The legacy of autonomy in American journalism. In Overholser, Geneva & Hall Jamieson, Kathleen (eds.) *Institutions of democracy: The press*. Oxford: Oxford University Press, pp. 384–399.

Grafstrm , Maria, & Windell, Karolina (2012). Newcomers conserving the old: Transformation processes in the field of news journalism. *Scandinavian Journal of Management*, 28(1), 65–76.

Greider, Gö an (2012). Makten från ovan. *Göteborgs-Posten*. Retrieved on July 25, 2021, from: https://www.gp.se/kultur/kultur/makten-fr%C3%A5n-ovan-1.662194.

Grosjean, Blandine (2014). La saga du Nouvel Obs: "On est des intellos, faut pas déconner!". Retrieved on May 14, 2020 from: https://www.nouvelobs.com/rue89/rue89-medias/20140317.RUE2707/la-saga-du-nouvel-obs-on-est-des-intellos-faut-pas-deconner.html.

Gruppo 24 Ore (2019) Media Room. Retrieved on December 2, 2019 from: https://www.gruppo24ore.ilsole24ore.com/it-it/media/

Guggenheim, M., & Potthast, J. (2012). Symmetrical twins: On the relationship between Actor-Network Theory and the sociology of critical capacities. *European Journal of Social Theory*, 15(2), 157–178.

Habermas, Jü gen (2006). Political communication in media society: Does democracy still enjoy an epistemic dimension? The impact of normative theory on empirical research. *Communication Theory*, 16(4), 411–426.

Hadenius, Stig, & Weibull, Lennart (1999). The Swedish newspaper system in the late 1990s: Tradition and transition. *Nordicom Review*, 20(1), 129–152.

Hallin, Daniel C. (1992). The passing of the "high modernism" of American journalism. *Journal of Communication*, 42(3), 14–25.

Hallin, Daniel C., & Mancini, Paolo (2004). *Comparing media systems: Three models of media and politics*. Cambridge: Cambridge University Press.

Hammerschmid, Gehard & Meyer, Renate E. (2005). New Public Management in Austria: Local variation on a global theme? *Public Administration*, 83(3), 709–733.

Harris, John F. & VandeHei, Jim (2007). *Mission statement*. Retrieved on May 10, 2020 from: https://www.politico.com/aboutus/missionstatement.html.

Haski, Pierre (2010). *Rue89 a 3 ans et bientôt une petite sœur, Revue89*. Retrieved on July 16, 2020 from: https://www.nouvelobs.com/rue89/rue89-medias/20100506.RUE6394/rue89-a-3-ans-et-bientot-une-petite-s-ur-revue89.html.

Haski, Pierre (2011). *Une augmentation de capital pour développer Rue89*. Retrieved on July 16, 2020 from: https://www.nouvelobs.com/rue89/rue89-medias/20110630.RUE3135/une-augmentation-de-capital-pour-developper-rue89.html.

Haski, Pierre (2012). Rue89 et Nouvel Obs : le mariage entre en vigueur. Retrieved on July 25, 2021 from: https://www.nouvelobs.com/rue89/rue89-making-of/20120107.RUE6924/rue89-et-nouvel-obs-le-mariage-entre-en-vigueur.html.

Hepp, Andreas, & Loosen, Wiebke (2021). Pioneer journalism: Conceptualizing the role of pioneer journalists and pioneer communities in the organizational re-figuration of journalism. *Journalism*, 22(3), 577–595.

Hermida, Alfred, & Young, Mary Linn (2019). From peripheral to integral? A digital-born journalism not for profit in a time of crises. *Media and Communication*, 7(4), 92–102.

Hervieux, Chantal, Gedajlovic, Eric, & Turcotte, Marie-France B. (2010). The legitimization of social entrepreneurship. *Journal of Enterprising Communities: People and Places in the Global Economy*, 4(1), 37–67.

Il Sole-24 Ore (2007). *Il Sole-24 Ore Group Profile*. Original title: *Il Sole-24 Ore. Profilo di Gruppo*. Milano, Italy: Il Sole-24 Ore S.p.A.

Jagd, Soren (2011). Pragmatic sociology and competing orders of worth in organizations. *European Journal of Social Theory*, 14(3), 343–359.

Jagd, Soren (2013). *Criticism and the emergence of novelty in organizations*. In Fifth International Symposium on Process Organization Studies: The Emergence of Novelty in Organizations, Chania, Greece.

Jarzabkowski, Paula, Matthiesen, Jane, & Van de Ven, Andrew H. (2009). Doing which work? A practice approach to institutional pluralism. In Lawrence, Tom, Suddaby, Roy & Leca, Bernard (eds.) *Institutional work: Actors and agency in institutional studies of organizations*. Cambridge: Cambridge University Press, pp. 284–316.

Jesuisunclown (2010, January 6). *Pierre Haski, Laurent Mauriac, et Pascal Riché, Rue89*. Retrieved on May 10, 2020 from: https://www.youtube.com/watch?v=ePAfh7zl_x0

Joerges, Berward, & Czarniawska, Barbara (1998). The qe stion of technology, or how organizations inscribe the world. *Organization Studies*, 19(3), 363–385.

Jones, Ron Nell Andersen (2011). Litigation, legislation, and democracy in a post-newspaper America. *Wash. & Lee Legal Review*, 68, 557–637.

Järventie-Thesleff, Rita, Moisander, Johanna, & Villi, Mikko (2014). The strategic challenge of continuous change in multi-platform media organizations: A strategy-as-practice perspective. *International Journal on Media Management*, 16(3–4), 123–138.

Kantar Sifo (2020). *Dagspress*. Retrieved on May 10, 2020 from: https://www.kantarsifo.se/rapporter-undersokningar/audit-rapporter.

Karppinen, Kari, & Moe, Hallvard (2016). What we talk about when talk about "media independence". *Javnost – The Public*, 23(2), 105–119.

Kennedy, Marie (2016). Vi ger oss inte trots att det är tufft. *Göteborgs-Posten*, October 8, pp. 202 1.

Kingsley, Patrick (2018). *Orban and His Allies Cement Control of Hungary's News Media*. Retrieved on May 9, 2020 from: https://www.nytimes.com/2018/11/29/world/europe/hungary-orban-media.html.

Kraatz, Matthew S., & Block, Emily S. (2008). Organizational implications of institutional pluralism. In Greenwood, Royston, Oliver, Christine, Sahlin, Kerstin, & Suddaby, Roy (eds.) *The Sage handbook of organizational institutionalism*. London: Sage Publications, pp. 243–275.

Lapidus, Arne (2010, April 10). Nu ritas svenska mediekartan om, *Kvällsposten*, pp. 32–33.

Latour, Bruno (1990). Technology is society made durable. *The Sociological Review*, 38, 103–131.

Latour, Bruno (2005a). From *Realpolitik* to *Dingpolitik*. Or how to make things public. In Weibel, Peter & Latour, Bruno (eds) *Making things public: Atmospheres of democracy*. Cambridge: MIT Press, pp. 4–31.

Latour, Bruno (2005b). *Reassembling the social: An introduction to actor-network-theory*. Oxford: Oxford University Press.

Latour, Bruno (2016). *Politiques de la nature: Comment faire entrer les sciences en démocratie*. Paris: La découverte.

Latour, Bruno & Woolgar, Steve (1979). *Laboratory life: The social construction of scientific facts*. Beverly Hills: Sage Publications.

Lehtisaari, Katja, Villi, Mikko, Gröl und, Mikko, Lindén, Carl Gustav, Mierzejewska, Bozena I., Picard, Robert, & Roepnack, Axel (2018). Comparing innovation and social media strategies in Scandinavian and US Newspapers. *Digital Journalism*, 6(8), 1029–1040.

Li, You (2019). The role performance of native advertising in legacy and digital-only news media. *Digital Journalism*, 7(5), 592–613.

Lindberg, Kajsa, Czarniawska, Barbara, & Solli, Rolf (2015). After NPM? *Scandinavian Journal of Public Administration*, 19(2), 3–6.

Lindén, Carl-Gustav & Tuulonen, Hanna (eds.) (2019). *News automation: The rewards, risks and realities of "machine journalism"*. Retrieved on July 25, 2021 from: https://cris.vtt.fi/en/publications/news-automation-the-rewards-risks-and -realities-of-machine-journl.

Lindgren, Håkan (2015). Medias intellektuella och moraliska kris, *Göteborgs-Posten*, March 1, 2015, pp. 61–62.

Lippmann, Walter (1922). *Public opinion*. New York: Harcourt, Brace.

Lögr en, Stefan (2012). Stampen fortsätter växa. Retrieved on May 10, 2020 from: https://www.gp.se/ekonomi/stampen-fortsätter-växa-1.694701.

Lundin, Kim (2015, November 5). Stampen tonar ned krishotet, Dagens Industri, p. 18.

Maares, Phoebe, & Hanusch, Folker (2020). Exploring the boundaries of journalism: Instagram micro-bloggers in the twilight zone of lifestyle journalism. *Journalism*, 21(2), 262–278.

Man, John (2010). *The Gutenberg revolution*. London: Random House.

Maras, Steve (2013). *Objectivity in journalism*. Cambridge: John Wiley & Sons.

Maugeri, Mariano (2003, November 8). La Nuova Sede del Sole 24-Ore. *Ventiquattro, Il Sole-24 Ore*, pp. 29–32.

Mauriac, Laurent (2010). Rue89 publies ses comptes 2010. Retrieved on July 25, 2021 from: https://www.nouvelobs.com/rue89/rue89-medias/20110419.RUE1906/rue89 -publie-ses-comptes-2010.html.

McChesney, Robert D. (2004). *The problem of the media*. New York: NYU Press.

McInerney, Paul-Brian (2008). Showdown at Kykuit: Field-configuring events as loci for conventionalizing accounts. *Journal of Management Studies*, 45, 1089–1116.

Mesny, Ann & Mailhot, Chantale (2007). The difficult search for compromises in a Canadian industry/university research partnership. *Canadian Journal of Sociology*, 32, 203–226.

Morozov, Evgeny (2012). A robot stole my Pulitzer. Retrieved on July 25, 2021 from: https://slate.com/technology/2012/03/narrative-science-robot-journalists -customized-news-and-the-danger-to-civil-discourse.html.

Nilsson, Åsa, & Weibull, Lennart (2010). Vad händer med läsningen av den stora morgontidningen i den nya medievärlden? In *SOM-rapport* (No. 47). Retrieved on July 25, 2021 from: https://som.gu.se/digitalAssets/1339/1339043345 -376-nilsson -o-weibull--gp.pdf.

Noam, Eli M. (ed.) (2016). *Who owns the world's media? Media concentration and ownership around the world*. Oxford: Oxford University Press.

Olander, Karin & Hofbaue, Catherine (2016, May 24). Rekonstruktö en vill rädda personalen. *Dagens Nyheter*, p. 8.

Ordine dei Giornalisti, Odg (1993). Charter of the journalist's duties. Original title: Carta dei doveri del giornalista. Retrieved on July 25, 2021 from: https://www.odg

.mi.it/sites/default/files/modulistica/cartade i_doveride lgi ornalista_-8 l uglio 1993 .pdf.

Patriotta, Gerardo, Gond, Pascal & Schultz, Fredrieke (2011). Maintaining legitimacy: Controversies, orders of worth and public justifications. *Journal of Management Studies*, 48, 1804–1836.

Pedroni, Marco (2015). "Stumbling on the heels of my blog": Career, forms of capital, and strategies in the (sub) field of fashion blogging. *Fashion Theory*, 19(2), 179–199.

Picard, Robert G. (ed.) (2002). *Media firms: Structures, operations, and performance*. Mahwah, NJ: Lawrence Erlbaum Associates.

Picard, Robert G. (2005). *Money, media, and the public interest*. Oxford: Oxford University Press.

Porlezza, Colin (2017). Under the influence: Advertisers' impact on the content of Swiss free newspapers. *Media and Communication*, 5(2), 31–40.

Power, Michael (1999). The audit society: Rituals of verification. *British Journal of Educational Studies*, 47, 92–93.

Radcliffe, Vaughan S. (1997). Competing rationalities in "special" government audits: The case of NovAtel. *Critical Perspectives on Accounting*, 8(4), 343–366.

Raviola, E. (2010). *Paper Meets Web. How the Institutions of News Production Works On Paper and Online*. Doctoral dissertation. Jökpi ng International Business School, DS 65, 2010.

Raviola, E. (2014). We have never been pure. Negotiations between journalism and business in newspaper organizations. In Pallas, Josef, & Strannegård, Lars (eds.) *Organizations and the media – organizing in a mediatized world*. London: Routledge, pp. 96–115.

Raviola, Elena (2017). Meetings between frames: Negotiating worth between journalism and management. *European Management Journal*, 35(6), 737–744.

Raviola, Elena (2019). Just like any other business or a special case? Framing excess in a Swedish newspaper group. In Czarniawska, Barbara & Lö gren, Orvar (eds.) *Overwhelmed by overflows?* Lund: Lund University Press, pp. 96–110.

Raviola, Elena & Dubini, Paola (2016). The logic of practice in the practice of logics: Practicing journalism and its relationship with business in times of technological changes. *Journal of Cultural Economy*, 9(2), 197–213.

Raviola, Elena & Norbäck, Maria (2013). Bringing technology and meaning into institutional work: Making news at an Italian business newspaper. *Organization Studies*, 34(8), 1171–1194.

Reed, Michael, & Anthony, Peter (1992). Professionalizing management and managing professionalization: British management in the 1980s. *Journal of Management Studies*, 29(5), 591–613.

Remy, Jaqe line (2016). *Le Nouvel Observateur, 50 ans de passion*. Paris: Pygmalion.

Renzo Piano Building Workshop (2004). *Il Sole-24 Ore New Building*. Original title: *Nuova Sede per Il Sole-24 Ore*. Genova, Italy: Renzo Piano Building Workshop.

Reporters Sans Frontières (n.d.). *Media Independence*. Retrieved on July 25, 2021 from: https://rsf.org/en/actions/media-independence.

Rice, Andrew (2010, May 12). Putting price on words. *New York Times Magazine*. Retrieved on July 25, 2021 from: https://www.nytimes.com/2010/05/16/magazine/16Journalism-t.html.

Rothman, Stanley, & Lichter, S. Robert (1987). Elite ideology and risk perception in nuclear energy policy. *American Political Science Review*, 81(2), 383–404.

Roudakova, N. (2017). *Losing Pravda: Ethics and the press in post-truth Russia*. Cambridge: Cambridge University Press.

Rue89 (2011). "Le Nouvel Observateur" et "Rue89" s'allient. Retrieved on July 25, 2021 from : https://www.nouvelobs.com/medias/20111221.OBS7270/le-nouvel -observateur-et-rue89-s-allient.html.

Santi, Pascal (2007, May 3). Des anciens de "Libération" créent un nouveau site d'information. *Le Monde*. Retrieved on July 25, 2021 from: https://www.lemonde.fr/ actualite-medias/article/2007/05/03/des-anciens-de-liberation-creent-un-nouveau -site-d-information904890_3236_.html.

Sarfatti Larson, Magali (1977). *The rise of professionalism: A sociological analysis*. Berkley, CA: University of California Press.

Schedler, K., & Proeller, I. (2002). The New Public Management: A perspective from mainland Europe. In McLaughlin, Kate, Osborne, Stephan P., & Ferlie, Ewan (eds.) *New Public Management: Current trends and future prospects*. London: Routledge, pp. 163–180.

Schneiderman, Daniel (2011). *Impasse89 ou Boulevard89?* Retrieved on July 25, 2021 from: https://www.arretsurimages.net/discussions/impasse89-ou-boulevard89.

Schudson, Michael (1981). *Discovering the news: A social history of American newspapers*. New York: Basic Books.

Schudson, Michael (1995). *The power of news*. Cambridge, MA: Harvard University Press.

Schudson, Michael (2001). The objectivity norm in American journalism. *Journalism*, 2(2), 149–170.

Schultz, Julianne (1998). *Reviving the Fourth Estate: Democracy, accountability and the media*. Cambridge: Cambridge University Press.

Scott, W. Richard (2008). Lords of the dance: Professionals as institutional agents. *Organization Studies*, 29(2), 219–238.

Serazio, Michael (2013). *Your ad here*. New York: NYU Press.

Smith, Anthony (1980). *Goodbye, Gutenberg: The newspaper revolution of the 1980s*. Oxford: Oxford University Press.

Somin, Ilya (1998). Voter ignorance and the democratic ideal. *Critical Review*, 12(4), 413–458.

Sourdès, Lucile (2013). La rédaction de Rue89 se mobilise contre "le changement du haute de la page". Retrieved on July 25, 2021 from : https://www.nouvelobs.com/ rue89/rue89-making-of/20131206.RUE0694/la-redaction-de-rue89-se-mobilise -contre-le-changement-du-haut-de-la-page.html.

Spiil (2016). Making enterprise in the press sector: The reasons for believing in it. Press release. Retrieved on June 1, 2019 from: http://www.spiil.org/20161221/ entreprendre-presse-raisons-d-y-croire-retour-7e-journ-e-de-presse-ligne.

Stampen (2009). *Annual Report* 2009. Gothenburg, Sweden: Stampen AB.

Stampen (2010). *Annual Report* 2010. Gothenburg, Sweden: Stampen AB.

Stampen (2011). *Annual Report* 2011. Gothenburg, Sweden: Stampen AB.

Stark, David (2009). Heterarchy: The organization of dissonance. *The sense of dissonance: Accounts of worth in economic life*. Princeton, NJ: Princeton University Press, pp. 1–34.

Stark, David (2017). For what it's worth. In Cloutier, Charlotte, Gond, Jean Pascal, & Leca, Bernard (eds.) *Justification, evaluation and critique in the study of organizations*. Research in Sociology of Organizations, nr 52. London: Emerald Publishing, pp. 383–397.

SVT (2015). UG-Referens: Tidningspelet. Retrieved on July 25, 2021 from: https:// www.svt.se/nyheter/granskning/ug/referens/ug-referens-tidningsspelet.

Syrén, Michael, Carlsson, Tomas & Thunborg, Peter (2016, May 26). Stampen-pampens lä: 74 miljoner. *Expressen*, p. 16.

Thévenot, Laurent (2001). Organized complexity: conventions of coordination and the composition of economic arrangements. *European Journal of Social Theory, 4*, 405425.

Thévenot, Laurent (2002a). Conventions of co-ordination and the framing of uncertainty. *Intersubjectivity in Economics*, 181–197.

Thévenot, Laurent (2002b). Which road to follow? The moral complexity of an "eqi pped" humanity. In Smith, Barbara H. & Weintraub, E. Roy (eds.) *Complexities: Social studies of knowledge practices*. Durham, NC: Duke University Press, pp. 53–87.

Thornton, Patricia H., & Ocasio, William (2008). Institutional logics. In Thornton, Patricia H., Ocasio, William, Greenwood, Royston, Oliver, Christine, Suddaby, Roy & Sahlin, Kerstin (eds.) *The Sage handbook of organizational institutionalism*. Thousand Oaks, CA: Sage Publishing, pp. 99–128.

Thornton, Patricia H., Ocasio, William, & Lounsbury, Michael (2012). *The institutional logics perspective: A new approach to culture, structure, and process*. Oxford: Oxford University Press.

Townley, Barbara (2002). The role of competing rationalities in institutional change. *Academy of Management Journal, 45*(1), 163–179.

Tuchman, Gaye (1973). Making news by doing work: Routinizing the unexpected. *American Journal of Sociology, 79*(1), 110–131.

Tuchman, Gaye (1978). *Making news: A study in the construction of reality*. New York: Free Press.

Tunstall, Jeremy (1971). *Journalists at work*. London: Constable.

Uppdragsgranskning (2015). *Tidningsspelet*. Retrieved on May 10, 2020 from: https://www.svt.se/nyheter/amne/UG_-T idningsspelet.

von Dohnanyi, Johannes, & Mö ler, Christian (2003). *The impact of media concentration on professional journalism*. Vienna, Austria: OSCE. Retrieved on May 14, 2020 from: https://www.osce.org/fom/13870?download=true

Vos, Tim P. & Singer, Jane B. (2016). Media discourse about entrepreneurial journalism: Implications for journalistic capital. *Journalism Practice, 10*(2), 143–159.

Wedel, Kristina (2015). *Historik*. Retrieved on May 10, 2020 from: https://info.gp.se/om-gp/historik/.

Weinshall, Matthew (2003). Means, ends, and public ignorance in Habermas's theory of democracy. *Critical Review, 15*(1–2), 23–58.

Westgårdh, Anders & Johnsson, Robert (2012). *Avstampet. Berättelse om en mediekoncern uppgång och framgång*. Gö eborg, Sweden: Stampen AB.

Wilde, Oscar (1891/1998). *The soul of man, and prison writings*. Oxford: Oxford University Press.

Wojdynski, Bartosz W., & Golan, Guy J. (2016). Native advertising and the future of mass communication. *American Behavioral Scientist, 60*(12), 1403–1407.

Index

Printed and bound by CPI Group (UK) Ltd, Croydon, CR0 4YY

16/04/2025

14658434-0005